RUTH VERDE ZEIN

CRITICAL
READINGS

LATIN AMERICA: THOUGHTS

Romano Guerra Editora
Nhamerica Platform

MANAGEMENT COORDINATION
Abilio Guerra, Fernando Luiz Lara and Silvana Romano Santos

CRITICAL READINGS
Ruth Verde Zein
Brasil 5

EDITOR
Abilio Guerra, Fernando Luiz Lara and Silvana Romano Santos

EDITORIAL STAFF
Silvana Romano Santos, Fernando Luiz Lara, Abilio Guerra
and Fernanda Critelli

EDITORIAL ASSISTANT
Fabiana Perazolo

GRAPHIC DESIGN
Maria Claudia Levy and Ana Luiza David (Goma Oficina)

FORMATTING
Fernanda Critelli

TRANSLATION
Anita Di Marco and Ann Puntch

TRANSLATION REVIEW
Ruth Verde Zein and Fernanda Critelli

Romano Guerra Editora

SÃO PAULO

AUSTIN

2019

RUTH VERDE ZEIN

CRITICAL
READINGS

8 FOREWORD

12 BACK TO
THE THINGS

66 AN ETHICAL PRAGMATIC CRITIQUE,
AN OPERATIVE AND REFERENCED THEORY

88 THE SYNTHESIS AS A STARTING
POINT AND NOT A FINISH LINE

102 WHEN DOCUMENTING
IS NOT ENOUGH

126 IT AIN'T
NECESSARILY SO…

154 BREUER AFFECTIONS,
BACK AND FORTH

174 HARD CASES

192 NULLA DIE
SINE LINEA

196 BRENNAND CHAPEL

202 MODERN TRADITION
AND CONTEMPORARY CULTURE

236 LATIN AMERICAN
CONTEMPORARY ARCHITECTURE

FOREWORD

In 2000 my first book *O lugar da crítica. Ensaios oportunos de arquitetura*, was published. It gathered some texts written as a journalist and architectural critic, during the last decades of the 20th century. And it ended a cycle and opened another: then, after twenty years of professional activities, I decided to fully embrace the academic world. In this century, being a professor and a researcher became my main activity. After another twenty years, this new book presents a part of my activities, collecting some unpublished and out-of-print texts.

The first part of this book brings forth some pedagogical texts. They were elaborated in the effort of practicing the teaching, the study and the research of architecture in a more conscious and critical way. Like every work that demands a lot of effort, but when it is finished, it passes almost unnoticed – especially when it is done right –, educational activities seems an inane activity, when in fact they are essential. I believe architectural education is provided by helping to learn and recognize the world's realities, in their cultural and human manifestations, especially those related to the built environment. To teach design is to create links with the relevant tradition as much as it is to enable its renovation, advancing to new and, hopefully, better paths. To teach how to research, especially in the field of architectural design – the subject that I'm mostly interested – is also a process of awareness of the knowledge that must be assimilated and transformed. It is also a demystification of *truths*, which must be requalified as *narratives* in order to make it possible to question them. These apparently abstract subjects that are quite real and concrete in the everyday teaching and research activities, are debated in the first four texts.

The second part of this book brings forth five texts considering some aspects on the subject of critical readings; or as I've renamed, and explained why in one of the texts, of *critical* and *referenced studies*. It presents a selection of projects and authors that I am very fond of, not because we are friends (though sometimes that is also true), but because their works tell me things that I would not be able to think or do by myself, and that is why I learn a lot by reading them in a deep and careful way. These writings do not intend to unveil some hidden truth behind those works and architects but instead, they just explain what they are to me. My spectrum of interests is obviously wider, but this book had room to accommodate just a few of such exercises.

In third and final part of the book there are two more broad and panoramic texts. The first one on brutalism, in this case, focused on the architecture of my hometown, São Paulo. It reverberates some of my extensive studies on the theme, which I've been studying since the 1980s until today, and will always be a personal subject of interest. The second text is about another subject that also deeply interests me: Latin American modern and contemporary architecture. I have chosen to place them last, knowing that they are inherently fragile, but in the hope that the indulgent reader would, by then, give me some leeway to practice some necessarily dated and finite generalizations. Despite their possible flaws, they do matter not as much for what they say, but mostly for how they were construed, or better, for the method I've used to write them: Through the accumulation, sifting and systematizing in a long-term process of acquiring an overall knowledge on things, facts, architectures, projects and cities. These texts were not born from some priori intellectual convictions, but after the determination of arranging, in a more or less didactic way, what I have learned along my way.

FOREWORD

I finish this brief foreword thanking the women that made this book possible: Silvana, Fernanda, Noemi, Anita. Friends, sisters, kind force that, I am sure, are helping to change the world for the better.

BACK TO THE THINGS

LEARNING FROM THE BUILDINGS

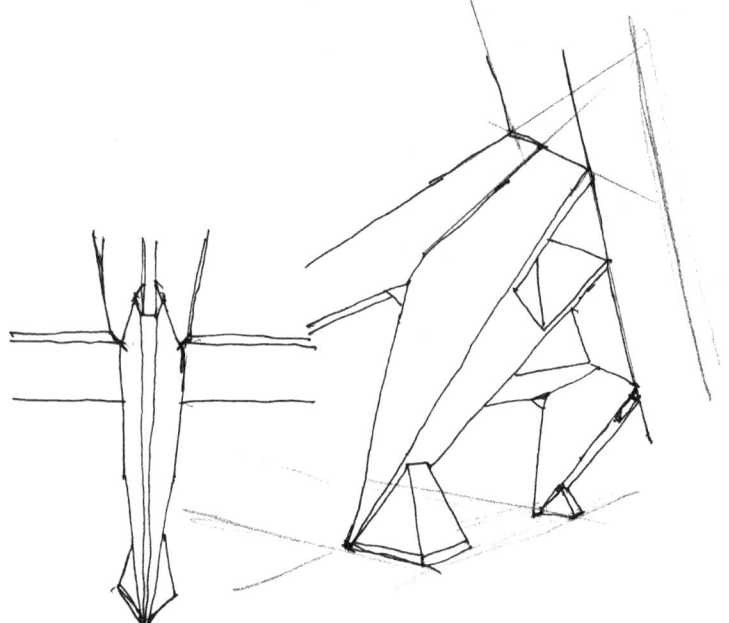

Anhembi Tennis Club, perspective of the structure, São Paulo SP.
Vilanova Artigas and Carlos Cascaldi, 1961. Drawing Ruth Verde Zein

The new generation has a splendid dose of vital force, the first
condition of any historical enterprise; that is why I have hope in
it. But at the same time I suspect that it completely lacks internal
discipline, without which its strength disaggregates and volatilizes:
That is why I do not trust it. Curiosity is not enough when doing
things; one needs mental rigor to become their owners.[1]

How to do a critical analysis of a building? I have often heard this
question, especially after lecturing in universities, congresses, and
conferences and after presenting my own close readings on modern
and contemporary Brazilian architecture buildings. The question
may seem superfluous, and the subject may not need further explanation. After all, a critical analysis, or a close reading of a building is
not exactly a novelty, numerous authors and dozens of professors do
exercise it every day. Even so the question frequently arises when I
also suggest the possibility, indeed the necessity, of using this kind
of practical-theoretical tool to open up some possibilities in the academic research field of architecture design. Again, that is a not a
new road, for it has already been traveled by many others, even if it
is still under construction. But anyway, the question usually arises
when I suggest that this kind of study, which has already been in use
for quite some time, is meant to become an indispensable methodological tool, helping to bridge up two connected, but still separated,

professional areas: Architecture design as a practice and architecture design as a research practice. And since the interest in the topic of critical analysis/close reading as a research tool in architectural design seems to be receiving a greater amount of attention, and it is being more frequently adopted by several researchers, perhaps it is in order to try and better understand its nature, and to systematize its scope and comprehensiveness.

Considering only my personal experience as a participant of several domestic and international academic events and associations, I dare say that there seems to be an increasing interest in the topics of *design research* and *critical readings*. That suggests the possibility of also increasing the interest in a most intriguing and utopic horizon, which is perhaps a chimera: The possibility of deeply, concertedly, systematically, and clearly connecting research and design, theory and design, critique and design. To put it in another way, that tool may represent an opportunity to better access and to link the architectural practice to other two realms that are supposedly also familiar to architects – critical reflection and theoretical thought; although they happen to result only in the best cases, sometimes quite unexpectedly, as a collateral byproduct of the act of design.[2]

So, would it be convenient, or even possible, to establish some simple and judicious method to help us, or primarily to guide young researchers, into a better way of studying and understanding the works of architecture? Should one consider critical analysis/close readings as a useful method to broaden architectural knowledge within the academic universe of architecture research, with possible repercussions on the architecture practice?

Evidently, any attempt to try and completely understand a work of architecture would be futile, a philosophically impossible task. But would it be possible to establish some clear, demonstrable, transferable, and plausible method to carry out a study, an analysis, a critical reading, a wider assessment of a building, solely or primarily based on the technical and professional knowledge that caused it to emerge, as concept and construct, in order to activate some substantiated and productive research path? If so, would it be worth suggesting some kind of checklist, or perhaps a few progressive steps to help those who are still novices at this task? Is it adequate to propose some kind of reference handbook, or a sort of *vade mecum*? Finally, or first of all, what does anyone understand by an analysis, or by a critical reading, or by a referenced critical recognition of a work of architecture?[3]

Let's begin with some brief definitions, or better yet, by establishing limits. The word analysis is defined in current dictionaries as a detailed examination of the elements and structure of certain phenomena; but it also means to separate and divide something, whether object or idea, into its constituent parts; in this case, perhaps in the illusion that the addition of the isolated knowledge of each part would result in the full knowledge of the whole. The first sense (a detailed examination) can be adopted here, but I absolutely do not accept the second definition: To reduce any architecture to a puzzle of parts in order to assure its overall understanding will probably foul up the comprehension of what is really important, which may be in all the parts, while simultaneously it is in no part at all. So, for now, it is better not to use the word *analysis* to describe the task at hand, and instead, to adopt a more extensive and somewhat more precise expression.

Thus I will restate the initial question in more precise terms, how I wish it had been framed to me: How does one achieve a certain level of referenced critical recognition of a building that allows for greater depth of its understanding, within an academic research, in order to... To what purpose, really? Well, this is perhaps an even more fundamental question. It has to be considered, it needs to be clearly enunciated and it must be fully answered.

I DO NOT UNDERSTAND THE PROCESS OF CRITICAL RECOGNITION OF A WORK OF ARCHITECTURE AS AN END IN ITSELF, BUT A TOOL TO OPEN OTHER DOORS.

That is why I insist on adding the word *referenced* to the complex definition above suggested, replacing the term *critical analysis*. This is a fundamental aspect, without whose consideration no satisfactory answers to the initial question will be achieved, for those asking the question, and even myself, may be inadvertently speaking about different subjects, different objectives and motives, different expectations, asking ourselves different things – even without being fully aware of that.

Speaking of motives, a brief digression is here necessary.

In his classic text "Ideologia modernista e ensino de projeto: duas proposições em conflito" (Modernist Ideology and Teaching of Architectonic Design: Two Conflicting Proposals),[4] Carlos Eduardo Dias Comas argues the need for critical referenced recognition of a broad repertory of works as an indispensable basis for the solution of design problems, and as an indispensable tool for tutoring design students in their design process. According to Comas, following the lessons of his masters Collin Rowe and Alan Colquhoun, deeper critical recognition of a wide repertory of works is not timely invoked just to illustrate a generic point, or erudition, nor just to get to know these works *in them*. But rather by being invoked they can illuminate the creative scenario in which one develops one's design, whether to warn us about occasional difficulties or to open up preferential possibilities that activate and/or counterbalance specific moments of a creative process. The catalyzing presence of the recognition of other works in one's design process is also a critical re-cognition, since it is the result and expression of some criteria (explicit or not) that induced us to make a selection, defining those works that are suitable or that we are interested in studying, *ad hoc* in this case. Therefore, it is referenced knowledge that goes both ways: Because I reference myself, and because my references seek it.

But would it be possible to try to re-cognize some architecture works in them? That is, in a non-referenced and thus absolute way? Would this perhaps be the situation encountered when the referenced critical recognition of a building is not suggested by the design process, but by the writing of a thesis, an article, a text, a class, a dissertation, i.e., when the task at hand is essentially academic and theoretical, and not professional? I believe not. Or better, here I propose to defend an opposite position: That every critical recognition of a building, even inside a theoretical appointment, is necessarily a referenced one, whether we are aware of that or not. And better be aware, for any naïve or unconscious approach to the subject is not adequate in a serious and meticulous academic task, for taking into account the processes and paths of our thoughts is an unavoidable and basic obligation at that. If that is so, the possibility of elaborating a generic *vade mecum*, able to be used in any case, will never be possible. Because first of all, one must begin by proposing a first question: Why do I want to better understand this building or this set of buildings? For what purpose am I invoking them?

There is another important second question to be proposed. If we are trying to establish, in an academic research, a list of possible elements to allow us to propose a *referenced critical recognition* of a building, it must be considered that such building was created by the current design methods of architecture professional field, i.e., it was originally designed mainly through non-verbal or non-textual elements, such as drawings, sketches, models, test models, etc. Thus, would it be possible, or even more correct, to propose a referenced critical recognition mostly, or exclusively, by employing such non-textual/verbal tools? Is it possible to completely dispense with the support of verbal and textual elements?

My position here is also contrary: It does not seem so. I defend it invoking at least two reasons. First, because it seems evident that architects do not dispense the aid of verbal and textual elements within the design process itself, and not just to explain or divulge it to third parties (when written or verbal explanations are customary). Secondly, because whenever a piece of critical recognition of a building is developed within the academy, it must be attentive to the *raison d' être* of academies. They are meant to be places for the dissemination and propagation of the knowledge produced by each of their members, who will validate or contest this knowledge; and after being proven and validated, this knowledge must be publicized to the world and put into use. As so, it is a fair reason to demonstrate the need of combining, when doing a referenced critical recognition, textual and non-textual elements, in order to help other people fully understand your study. After all, not everyone has or needs to have the proper training to fully comprehend architect's non-verbal language, or by extension, any professional field jargon. However, the vast majority of people will be able to comprehend well-argued verbal texts, supported to a greater or lesser degree by non-textual elements. This motive – the public interest and the need to be clear and communicative – is in my opinion sufficient to confirm the need for us to employ textual and non-textual elements in a referenced critical recognition of a building, especially when such study is being elaborated inside an academic study. We should not feed the illusion of being self-sufficient nor should we isolate ourselves. If we have something to say, it is our duty to be clear when telling it to everyone: Our peers, young novices, interested laypeople, other people connected to our research field etc.

Moreover, in explaining ourselves, in renouncing the pretentiousness of imagining that our area of knowledge is ineffable, and in being willing to be clear and communicative, we can open up the possibility of being challenged – which is, in principle, the appropriate condition of intelligent life in the academic debate. This is another basic point that needs to be accepted and that differentiates the professional practice of architecture from the professional practice of research in architecture. The alleged ineffability of the architectonic tasks can be tolerated in professional life whenever the clients are fully satisfied with the results. But in the academic research field *the client* is an indeterminate open collective, and thus it cannot by definition accept such incommunicability.

ALL INEFFABLE KNOWLEDGE MAY BE VALUABLE TO THOSE WHO HAVE IT, BUT SINCE IT IS NON-TRANSFERABLE IT FAILS IN THE MISSION OF BEING PUBLICIZED, SHARED, RESPONDED OR ENDORSED;

and of eventually benefitting a broader community – the *raison d'être* of any research. Lastly, but no less importantly, we need to be clear in order to be understood by people that belong to other academic research fields who, whether we like it or not, have also a say on the quality and pertinence of our research and on defining whether it will be accepted and validated. In other words, we must be straightforward because we also need to clearly communicate our efforts to the agencies that regulate academic life and set the standards for the assessment of the productivity of our lives as researchers.

So an important step of a possible check list (that I am not going to propose) is to endorse the double textual/non-textual nature of these kinds of studies: A piece of referenced critical recognition of an architectural work would certainly have to deal in every step of the way with non-verbal/non-textual representation and study devices (drawings, diagrams, sketches, designs, etc.) as well as it will necessarily have to deal with verbal and/or textual forms. More precisely, with everything the verbal as well as non-verbal forms carry: More or less abstract concepts and ideas, pertinent to the subject in a total or in a tangential way.[5]

While it is in development, or when it is being deepened and completed, a study proposing a referenced critical recognition of a building from an architectural standpoint cannot avoid but interfacing with a broad range of other parallel disciplines and adjacent knowledge, without which it would be impossible to qualify and correctly comprehend the network of complexities that may be found at the heart of all architectural works, especially when dealing, as it will be more frequently the case, with exemplary, canonical or significant cases. Therefore, it is convenient to keep in mind that the main focus and starting point for a referenced critical recognition of an architectural work will always be, by free definition and free choice of method, architectonic. The hypotheses, descriptions, considerations, developments and conclusions of a referenced critical study of a chosen architectonic work that one aspires to better recognize and appreciate (for the author's particular reasons, that should be explained at some point of the text) is necessarily born and is primarily fed on the knowledge and parameters of architectural disciplinary knowledge. In order to better do it one must adopt an intransigent stance pro reviewing the building in its essential architectonic conception, as a result of a design process that brought it to life, but from which the building has paradoxically freed itself at the moment it came into the world.[6]

By insisting on the need to focus the study of architecture works primarily through the architecture discipline knowledge it may look like as if we are in search of its roots, its origin, or its concrete manifestation that is apparently free of all bonds, ties, and connections. But in fact that is not the intention, nor that is possible to fully occur at any time.

It is impossible to perform a close reading, or a referenced critical recognition, of a work of art or architecture by disregarding the fact that it is already wrapped in an aura. It is impossible to remain completely free of the influence of this aura and to aspire to attain the pure *object in itself* as if it could be understood devoid of all the overlapping layers of meaning that were previously imposed there by us or others. Even when dealing with a completely new building, one cannot avoid viewing it with the biases that shape our vision, which is never innocent, even when it is not consciously reflexive. It will never be possible to eradicate the *crusts* that for better or worse are aggregated to the object, sometimes enmeshed in a nearly inextricable manner, even though in fact they were juxtaposed over time by authors, users, commentators etc. Admitting that, it is better to start the critical reading by accepting that these layers are ever-present and the subject is a complex entity. That is exactly why we need to invest in a certain effort to *denaturalize* these layers, by peeling them off, and by refusing to unadvisedly accept them as substitutes for the buildings themselves; even when it is inevitable that we use them as a basis to comprehend it, while, in the process, we strive to recognize, refine or contest these crusts.

Abandoning once and for all the idea that it is possible to produce a critical reading in itself, it is worth understanding that the effort of creating a close reading, or of a referenced critical recognition of an architectural work cannot avoid being a methodological proposition, a means to achieve an end, which is the purpose of our journey. And the knowledge thus produced will never be *pure*, but the hybrid and synergistic result of the association between our free and creative actions, interacting with the building (or buildings) that we have chosen to appreciate, to dedicate our time and effort to study and comprehend.

The reason to do a referenced critical recognition of any work of architecture is to arrive at an objective that we have previously established, whether or not in a conscious way, which will be clearly stated by asking the other basic fundamental question (why someone wants to do this task). Sooner or later, such question must be clearly formulated, in each and every case, in order to allow the entire process to be clear, and to allow it to be verified by the author and by others, in order to confirm its quality, its rigor and its consistency.

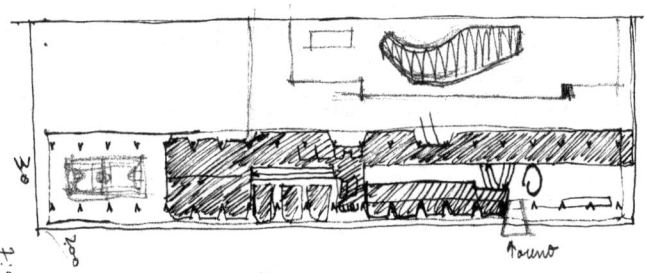

Anhembi Tennis Club, floor plan, São Paulo SP. Vilanova Artigas and Carlos Cascaldi, 1961. Drawing Ruth Verde Zein

Naturally it can happen – it almost always happens –, that during the process the questions change, are refined, are made more precise, and are transformed. The initial question does not have to be omniscient, it does not and cannot be expected to contain all the answers a priori, or else it would be neither a question nor a research, but a mere reiteration of some previous knowledge, which is in fact neither being expanded or tested. The question (or questions) can be called as hypothesis, but it may also be named, in a manner that is perhaps more pertinent to the case, as the concept of the project, in this case, the research project. Or it can be called intuition, or a glimpse, or whatever other names seem appropriate. What should not be done is to assume that it is necessary to begin by already knowing where one will arrive, because it does not work that way: As in the design process, knowledge is not there beforehand, but it is constructed during the process, in a non-linear way, with ups and downs, possibly arriving at dead ends which can be critically perceived, impelling us to retake the subject by other routes, and so on. The process of referenced critical recognition of a building is essentially a reflexive process, as much as the design process is.[7]

In other words, and as proposed here, the attempt to do a referenced critical recognition of a work of architecture, or a close reading, or its *analysis* (using the term only in the first sense described above) will start from some precise and chosen angle, which will both illuminate and limit our reading. During the process this focus will be revised time and again, whenever necessary and appropriate, reformulating the starting question and eventually even re-proposing either the question or the piece of architecture that we have chosen to be studied; for it could happen that the process enlightens our understanding and we realize that the object at issue might not be the best option to try and to respond our questions.

This type of work is by definition endless. But it may be managed, and considered to be sufficient: Not because the researcher has exhausted the possibilities of extracting knowledge out of the reading, but because one has already reached some established goals. Not because one has arrived at the truth, but because now it is possible to try out a plausible response, which now is ready to be expounded to a broader community. And ideally, within this community, called academic, our attempts will arouse some debate that will, in the best cases, help us refine our process of critical recognition, our ideas and our conclusions.

Be that as it may, neither are referenced critical recognitions of architectural works something unheard of. Many authors postulate their existence, under these or other names, and/or exercise this task in various ways, with more or less interesting, complete or consistent contributions. There is no pretension of inaugurating here a novel field, but just to discuss some of its premises with more detail and clarity.

Even though a work of architecture cannot be read by reducing it into some relatively simple items (in fact, there will be no checklist!), a building can be symbolically compared to a vector resulting from the geometrical summation of various internal and external forces that help shape it. These forces can be for example: A brief to attend/geometry of spaces; geographical and cultural site of its location/relationship to a place and surroundings; materials and techniques that can be employed/constructive and technological results; architectonic precedents which one wishes to prioritize or deny/formal and constructive emphases that are chosen as highlights. One can continue to list other items, basic but no less indispensable. The items listed above are just some examples, and are not meant to exhaust the subject. They may be useful because they are almost always present in any close reading, and may be taken as a starting point, at least by young researchers who wish to become initiated in the subject, and eventually the researcher will enrich the list by including or excluding others items, according to the reading aims and interests. These and other items look like simple neutral parameters, but they are not, nor can they be. In their apparent simplicity they can be considered with more or less depth and erudition, and eventually produce a referenced critical recognition of great complexity and richness. To achieve this goal, it is necessary to work hard in a persistent, extended, demanding way, as is true for anything in life that intend to be serious and achieve high quality results.

In any case, as a practical suggestion, it is a good idea to begin by a description of the building. A description may be considered as the near zero point of critique, but without it, the critique may not be able to exist.[8] No one runs a marathon without first having assiduously trained in some less extenuating races. Considering that, the parameters suggested above (and many others) can serve at least to exercise an initial reading, or as a training. It is also very important to amplify the knowledge and to exercise the correct application of specific and precise technical language appropriated to the case: Knowing how to handle and use the proper vocabulary helps us learn to see, apprehend and understand what one sees – and eventually, see what is not immediately seen, but could be manifested through your reading. After seeing and understanding what is there and what could be there, one can manage to know how to explain it, and eventually to know how to teach seeing it, and finally, when and if necessary, to know how to apply what one has learned in many other different ways.

It is important to notice that these items should not be adopted a priori as an abstract list, to be dissected in a point-by-point study: That would be an *analysis* as stated in the above discarded definition, and will tend to dispense or unduly substitute a proper and thorough study of the building. On the contrary, what matters is not the list but the buildings, they are the starting point of the reading, not their parts, nor the abstract items. Buildings condense in a complex and usually contradictory manner all the items that we propose to study, and others as well, and no checklist of items or aspects we are interested in learning about is able to substitute the buildings themselves. Due to the immeasurable conceptual density of the buildings and their architectonic complexity, their referenced critical recognition cannot be reduced to a handful of simple explications; which is right and just, since no architecture is the result of simple explanations. And if all that were easy, none of us would be here: The fun of all of this is its difficulty.

The items listed above, although basic, are obviously not the only possible ones. Defining which aspects should be considered, which to include or eliminate when doing a close reading is a deliberated decision, i.e., it is a choice based on some criteria, which in turn results in the consideration and comprehension of the initial question: The one that defines where we want to go, and why.

These chosen aspects or criteria can activate interdisciplinary connections whenever they are indispensable to the referenced critical recognition that we propose, or according to the references we adopt as the basis for our exploration. Notice that the term *activate* was intentionally used in the above paragraph, meaning that the kind of *critical reading* or *referenced critical recognition* or *close reading* of a building or any work of architecture here discussed does not begin from some interdisciplinary conceptual presuppositions, but could make use of them whenever necessary, but only when the criteria, as defined by the initial question, require them.

There is a subtle but powerful distinction between a reading that assumes extra-architectonic parameters as an priori basis, and another that does not shy away from also using extra-architectonic parameters, but only when they become relevant. What is here proposed, the subject of this text is the second situation. As above-mentioned, the key point of this proposal, its limit or its nature, it that a *critical reading*, or a referenced critical recognition of a building must not lose sight of a very simple, but radical fact. That architecture is born, grows and manifests itself in the world through creative human efforts which in bringing it into concrete form, takes as parameters for its definition and existential confirmation primarily the dictates of its disciplinary logic, that coordinates and synthesizes what is needed and what is necessary.

As such, architecture encompasses a disciplinary field in itself and is not reducible to a mere *consequence*, let alone cause, of pre-existing injunctions of the physical, social, economic, political environment; even though it is always necessarily to establish several links and connections with all these and other transdisciplinary fields.[9] In other words, under the terms here proposed, this kind of close reading is born from the buildings and grows into other directions, when necessary, and not vice-versa.[10]

The resolve to accept the buildings, the works of architecture, as the main basis for an academic study in architecture and design does not exclude, but rather makes it imperative as an indispensable foundation, to define the terms to which the study subscribes and in which it supports itself – as for example, the temporal, geographic, typological, and other perspectives that are adopted. It does not obviate the need to work on the subject in a systematic or *scientific* manner. This last term (scientific) is frequently questioned or misunderstood in the debates in our field. But it is neither mysterious nor complicated, and can be properly applied to the architectural research field, al least in its essentially methodological meaning. A study that activates a process beginning with an initial hypothesis, or with a more or less interpretative question can be considered scientific when it defines the means and tools it will use to verify the question, explicitly selects a method to allow its confirmation, and finally closes the argument with an unequivocal (or at least plausible) demonstration of its verification. Bearing in mind that

> the modalities and degrees of proof or confirmation of a theory in order to be declared or accredited as a *scientific theory* are not defined based on a single criterion: Manifesting the truth of a psychological or economic [*or architectonic, author's remark*] theory requires completely different means of proof [...] and the degrees of confirmation required are also different.[11]

And by proving an hypothesis of a study in such a volatile environment as the human creativity is perhaps not to make it in a flawless way, but it is enough to increase its plausibility and consistency. In this sense, there is nothing to prevent us from accepting that an academic study in architecture and design that uses the tool (or the *quasi* method) of critical analysis or close reading or referenced critical recognition of a building can be scientific.

Instead of continuing this text in a generic and abstract manner – which in my point view is absolutely not what I want to do –, I will briefly quote the contribution of some other authors to this subject. To conclude the text, I will exemplify how I have applied these ideas to my studies on various occasions. The examples of other authors are not meant to be exhaustive, but

Anhembi Tennis Club, transverse sections, São Paulo SP. Vilanova Artigas and Carlos Cascaldi, 1961. Drawing Ruth Verde Zein

random and referenced: I invoke them here because they were useful to me, but they in no way exhaust the subject. Even so, I believe that their contributions can also be of use to other people.

In addition to the above mentioned Comas and to the indispensable reference of Rowe and Colquhoun, I am personally greatly indebted to the conceptual contribution of the Argentinian historian, critic and architecture theorist Marina Waisman (1920-97). Considering her many texts, I would highlight some excerpts from her book, *El Interior de la Historia* (Inside History). Although this book aim is to describe the discipline of architectural historiography, in its first part Marina sets out clear perspectives for investigation and research in architecture in general, treating dense concepts such as history, historiography, narratives, durations etc., in a precise and clarifying manner, characterizing the specificities of the histories of art and architecture through concepts such as monument, document, and others further themes of great importance to architectural research. Her major contributions to the theme discussed here are especially in chapter 4 ("History, Theory, Critique") and chapter 5 ("Reflection and Praxis"), and here I quote some of its most clarifying excerpts:

History, theory and critique are three modes of reflecting on architecture, that are intimately interlaced and have often been confused in the past; they are differentiated by their methods and objectives. Moreover, they fulfill distinct functions in architectonic thought and praxis.[12]

Praxis provides the objects of reflection, and in turn reflection provides the concepts that guide praxis. [...] On the other hand, although the objects of reflection come from reality, they do not directly or obviously reveal the problems they contain; it is through reflection that we will find out what is there to discover, by revealing problems and questions that underline factual reality.[13]

Naturally, Marina Waisman also is indebted to her masters, especially Enrico Tedeschi (1910-78), an Italian architect residing in Argentina, with whom she studied and collaborated as a colleague in teaching and research. Tedeschi was a professor in Tucumán and Mendoza and was the author of the beautiful School of Architecture building, designed at the same time he published his book *Teoria de La Arquitectura*[14] (1962; third expanded edition, 1972), in which according to Josep Maria Montaner, "[he] proposes a pedagogical renewal based on the theory of design."[15] The fundamentals, with which Tedeschi proposed to establish a theory of architecture, even though they have more to do with teaching than research, have also greatly contributed to the study here proposed.

> The factors that have greatest importance in the design cannot be established in a fixed normative manner: Everything is a matter of relationships. [...] All questions, the numerous [questions] that the study of a design generates do not have single, eternal, categorical answers [...] Obviously, there are practical adjoining problems that are relatively easy to define [such as dimensions, etc.], but aside from these limits, the solution is totally free. Thus the need for critical reasoned focus on the part of architects which permits them to establish for each case a correct valuation of the factors that intervene in their designs and their relationships.[16]

**BACK TO
THE THINGS**

Critic preparation can be achieved only in one way: By examining and studying the works in which one seeks to recognize how the information from the design were understood and valorized by the architects. That is, transferring random experiences to our own work by means of meditated, detailed examination that should be repeated many times in order to become conscious of all the elements that participate in the design and in their transformation into a work of architecture.[17]

Reaffirmed here is the importance not of accumulating knowledge, but achieving a work method [...] In this way the collaboration of the studies of the theory of architecture in the design process becomes more concrete.[18]

I proceed with some other Argentinean references, now contemporary ones, that corroborate the perception our theme here is actually a present-day conceptual concern that is being manifested in different ways, in varied places and with possibly distinct, but sufficiently close, definitions.

Ignácio Lewkowicz and Pablo Sztulwark published a small but precious book, *Arquitectura plus de sentido: notas ad hoc* (architecture plus sense: Remarks ad hoc). According to the authors the term *plus* "is ambiguous and that is not so bad." The book explores various plus dimensions to help thinking about contemporary architectonic culture situation. The first part chapters have suggestive names and intriguing content: "The field of sense," "the architectonic subject," "a reflection on the object," and "the intellectual function." The second part chapters deal with context and design concepts, and the third proposes reflections on the contemporary city, themes explored in a following book by Sztulwark, *Ficciones de lo Habitar* (Housing Fictions). From the fourth chapter of the first part, I've extracted an absolutely exemplary dialectical proposition of the case in point in this text; although it is quite rhetorical, this excerpt helps clarify some points with certainty.

A work of architecture can be conceived, construed or registered as a thought in two ways: It can be effected as a performed thought, or it can be conceived as a thought in action. The difference is tiny, but essential. If the work is the outcome of a thought, then it is the pure expression of a previous meaning: On the one hand there is a thought; on the other its implementation, which would be the passing into action of what was potentially contained in the thought. Nothing is added; something that had already been created on the intelligible realm becomes reality. The other possibility is that the work can be conceived as a thought in action, i.e., that the initial

> thought, the reflection that guides the design and the decision,
> gives it place to an architectonic object. This object is precisely
> architectonic because it is in excess in relation to the thought
> that originated it. That is, the effect is irreducible to its cause and
> the thought does not contain in itself the entire doing.[19]

It is also worth highlighting another illuminating sentence from this book: "This book argues that if there is no reflection in architecture key, it is not because it is redundant, but simply because it is lacking. And that absence is noticeable."[20]

The quotes above seem to echo an important lesson from a fundamental text written by Francesco Dal Co, "Criticism and Design"[21] where the author establishes the status of critical independence and liberty of action for the researcher in the face of the work in study and in the face of the work creators and/or the circumstances that saw its emergence. With that, Dal Co dismounts the trap of understanding architecture as a mere consequence of...

> The appearance of a thing, rather than revealing mechanically
> the ideology of its production, exists simply as the place
> where its absolute autonomy from the act which produced
> it is revealed [...And thus] it can only be measured, read, and

known, if it is seen as autonomous of all those *realities* to which traditional historiography, in general, and architectural ideology, in particular, have always tried to tie it back.[22]

Some recent books can be considered as exemplary references for critically referenced studies of architecture works, even when they propose them under other names – such as *close reading*. This is the case of Peter Eisenman's book, a confirmed disciple of Collin Rowe who has, even more than his master, always taken a radical position in favor of extreme disciplinary autonomy. The book *Ten Canonical Buildings 1950-2000*[23] is radical and controversial and certainly does not please everyone, something that probably gives its author great pleasure. Regardless of whether or not it is possible to accept the full content of Eisenman studies in this book, his method of displaying the analytical designs (or diagrams) that accompany the text can be of interest to nourish a conceptual and methodological base for those who wish to undertake similar studies.

As a counterpoint, one can refer to another referential and exemplary book, *Los Hechos de La Arquitectura* (The Facts/Accomplishments of Architecture) by the Chilean architects Fernando Perez Oyarzun, Alejandro Aravena, and José Quintanilla. In one of the book's initial essays Aravena states:

BACK TO THE THINGS

Considering a history of architecture that had overly insisted on the formal components of the architectonic object, we propose a change in emphasis, without ever suspending the discipline's artistic dimension. What we propose is to shift the focus of our attention from an architecture viewed as a formal architectonic fact/accomplishment (judging the coherence of the internal syntax of the object), to one founded in architectonic facts/accomplishments (verifying the situations that the object is capable of articulating). This means here to stop looking at the formal properties of the form and start seeing something that may be called their vital properties.[24]

> I agree: But perhaps we are dealing more with a question of emphasis than choice, i.e., the famous this and that instead of this or that. In any case the three parts of this book are exemplary because they contain at least three distinct dimensions for a referenced critical reading and study of architecture works. Initially, some introductory essays address general issues and concepts; in the second part there are twenty examples of close readings, arranged more or less in the chronological order of the works design, beginning with the Parthenon and concluding with the Yale Center for British Art by Louis Kahn (including two Chilean and one Brazilian work, the Ministry of Health

and Education building). These short focused essays with illustrations, photographs and analytic sketches explore, in each case, some precise architectonic issue. The last part of the book includes a brief anthology of theoretical texts from eleven architects, including Vitruvio, Alberti, Laugier, Boullée, Durand, Ruskin, Viollet-Le-Duc, Le Corbusier, Mies, Gropius and, once again, Kahn. The book modestly intends to serve as a reading for freshmen students, but it is organized in such a way that even erudite readers can greatly appreciate its contribution. Here follows another excerpt from Aravena's initial essay:

It is the architectural facts/accomplishments that establish what we could call the architecture's own reality plane [...] Its verification allows us to rest with some certainty on the reality of the discipline, so often threatened to be dissolved into the pure naturalness of social life or into other disciplines and domains. Its verification allows us to be motivated, as architects, for this degree of simultaneous care and security that we call rigor. [...] If reality is to be observed, the architectonic facts/accomplishments are to be formulated.[25]

Other contemporary bibliographical references can be called upon to contribute to the theme here expounded, however the objective of this article is not to exhaust the subject, but to open perspectives.

Naturally, and contrary to popular wisdom, it is easier done than said. The initial question – how to do critical analysis of a building? – is perhaps plainer: It may not be calling for a method, just for an example. That is why it is convenient to present as well some practical exercises of close readings, or referenced critical recognition of some works. I will choose to do it here by commenting about some studies that I have been proposing, over the last decade, concerning some modern *paulista*[26] houses. The aim is not to repeat the ideas that I have already written, and may be read in other publications, but to use them to explain some methodological issues and corroborate the validity, range, flexibility and interest of the idea of a *referenced critical recognition*.

'PAULISTA' HOUSES: TRANGRESSIVE READINGS

Critique is analysis – a critique that does not analyze may be more comfortable, but cannot aspire to be fecund. [...] I don't understand critics without conscience. Science and consciousness, these are the two main principles to exercise a critique [...] Critics must be independent – independent in everything and from everything.[27]

The greatest difficulty to study the works of *paulista* architects such as João Batista Vilanova Artigas and Paulo Mendes da Rocha is that in these cases the aggregated crusts weigh tons, as anyone who tries to approach them in an independent manner knows.[28]

In my master's thesis, dedicated to a thorough reading of 42 houses designed by Paulo Mendes da Rocha,[29] I found it necessary to try and understand why our local *intelligentsia*, then and today, seems to dislike and to discourage any sort of critical architectonic reading of architecture works, preferring instead political, sociological, economic and other, approaches – a bias which invariably takes the readings away from the works themselves. I raised the hypothesis that this aversion was partially due to some *interdictions* that were set in place during the 1950s and were exacerbated in the 1960s-70s, which can be tracked back to a narrow critical reading of some of Vilanova Artigas' writings.

In some of his earlier texts Artigas displays an attitude of deep and consistent philosophical doubt, first expressed in "Os caminhos da arquitetura moderna"[30] (Modern Architecture Paths); a doubt whose broadest meanings were clarified by the posthumous publication of the master's late commentaries on the subject. Artigas' well-known question is formulated as: "Where are we? Or what should we do? Wait for a new society and continue to do what we do, or abandon the architect's tasks, since they take us in a direction hostile to the people, and launch ourselves fully into the revolutionary struggle?"[31] This question seems to sum up the tension between his political party engagement and his rejection of the aesthetic sectarianisms espoused by the conservative factions of the Communist Party, aligned with social realism guidelines that prioritized "art by the people for the people," but frequently adopted a narrow folklorist attitude, something Artigas as a conscious artist cannot accept, for it would be, in his words, the "denial of history."[32] At the end of "Os caminhos da arquitetura moderna" Artigas proposes to adopt a "critical attitude in the face of reality," that instead of denying the modern architecture he was fond of, sought to connect it with the "Brazilian roots of the universe," a Moacyr Felix catchphrase he also quotes. To reconcile it all, he never accepts nor allows the mere possibility of highlighting any non-local origin of the concepts and forms eventually present in modern Brazilian architecture, seeing that as a confession of dependence[33] – *ipso facto*, favoring the disconnection between local and international architectonic culture.

On the other hand, and in counterpoint, he holds to the absolute independence of the designers: "Architecture claims for itself a limitless freedom regarding formal use. A kind of liberty that only respects its internal logic as art."[34] In between the intransigence of not admitting to discuss *influences*, and the liberality of allowing their pervasiveness there remains a deliberately non-qualified void. That occurs because any creation never comes from nothing, and the creator is free to take for him/herself anything, re-elaborating, re-creating, accepting and rejecting any references that seem appropriate, assuming them in total or partially, or not, and changing them, at any time. A creative attitude exemplified by Artigas himself when he comments, on rare selected occasions, his own work.[35]

Artigas' doubt is resolved, according to Fuão, in a

frenetic search to create through architecture the image of a national identity, and against the international movement that was the same throughout the world. An immediate correlation between architectonic image and national culture.[36]

But that is not an incoherent, slippery or uncomfortable position, as Fuão suggests in the same text. On the contrary, Artigas position was a logical consistent consequence of the domineering political premises of that time, in the framework of the ideological disputes of 1950s-70s Cold War. Today, in the absence of that solid ground of antagonistic and excluding certainties, these debates became anachronistic, leaving only the master's perplexity and the stubbornness of his self-proclaimed disciples in enforcing, in an almost neurotic way, some ahistorical, acritical, strict, and sectarian interdiction obstructing the possibility of a broader, critical and open reading of *paulista*/ Brazilian works from an architectonic point of view; which of course, will touch the sore point of the references, or in a more controversial word, the influences.

Having said that, what is the sense of choosing to do a referenced critical recognition of some of the residences designed by Vilanova Artigas and Paulo Mendes da Rocha?

My question has always been: How does one design in architecture? But instead of asking the architects I prefer to interrogate their works, which always seemed more eloquent, precise, and friendly than their authors: Although mute, the buildings are perennially true. That is why I try critically reading them: Because I want to design better. If I chose to do some close readings of the works of Vilanova Artigas and Mendes da Rocha it is not only because they are a part of my life and education as architect but also because they are exceptional, controversial, dense and with a high degree of complexity. This in principle allows me to learn a lot from each of them.[37] Although houses are not the preferred subject of debate for those architects' generation – more for ideological than architectonic reasons – nevertheless they did not renounce to design them, and did that in an excellent manner.

As they are relatively small works, they allow for more compact readings and their apparent simplicity is a stimulating challenge, especially when one manages to lift the veils in order to observe even a minimal part of their complexities and contradictions.

In these readings I am always interested in understanding the controversial, difficult and *dangerous* issue of the influences dealt with and transformed by the act of designing. References and influences that must certainly exist because nothing comes from nothing and because even intuition is not exercised in a vacuum, but based on the knowledge of notable precedents applicable to the case, as Comas states.[38]

The subject of influences, or in the case of architecture, the choice of notable precedents that help inform the design, was treated in more detail in my doctoral dissertation,[39] and I quote:

In the São Paulo panorama, the explicit acceptance or any attempt at understanding and analyzing these influences is complicated by the fact that this type of approach is always received with a high degree of aversion [...] The reasons for this rejection, until a short while ago, were fundamentally of political and ideological order, and were connected especially to the theme of affirming a "national identity." [... But] this rejection also derives inevitably from the agony of artistic creation. As

Harold Bloom clarifies, "influence is a metaphor which implies
a framework of relationships, imagistic, temporal, spiritual,
psychological – all ultimately of a defensive nature."[40] Influence is
fundamental to creation in some way, but at the same time it must
be denied: "To arrive later, in cultural terms, is never acceptable to
a great writer" or to any artist, architects included. Influences thus
become, according to Bloom, "a stimulating burden," their denial
and overcoming them is one of the hidden motors of creation.[41]

> I have never understood quite well why the subject of influences would be *dangerous* (as my former *paulista* professors claimed), but that became clearer thanks to Bloom's warning. Understanding influences comes too close to the agonizing process of creation and rattles the foundation of the very basis for the supposed need of modern architects to be invariably *original*. In this sense, approaching this subject would be almost like a violation of intimacy, or so it is viewed in our professional world, so satisfied it is with the lack of critique as much as it affirms to want it. Even so the subject interests me since it is the best way to allow me to get closer to my long-lasting first question, "how do you design in architecture?" Nowadays, I don't believe in the possibility of ready definitive answers to this question, and I very much doubt those who intend to dogmatically propose them. Over time my approach to this subject became more

cautious and precise. Today at best I try and comprehend some aspects, not always nor necessarily the most fundamental ones, of the intimate creative process of design in architecture, and the most I manage to do is to suggest some connections. Paradoxically this seems to be sufficient to design and to tutor how to design, while readings accumulated and experiences succeed, more in a geometrical than in a simple addition.

I won't copy here the close readings I have done elsewhere, just suggest something of my *modus operandi*, or some of the texts methodological aspects.

In my articles, "Concretismo, concretão, neo-concretismo, algumas considerações e duas casas de Artigas"[42] (Concretism, Concrete, Neo-Concretism, Some Reflections and Two Houses by Artigas) and "Artigas Pop-Cult: considerações sobre a cabana primitiva, a casa pátio e quatro colunas de madeira"[43] (Artigas Pop-Cult: Reflections About the Primitive Hut, the Patio House and Four Wood Columns), I explore possible connections between the works of Vilanova Artigas and Brazilian and international art movements, contemporaneous to his works. In each case other issues timely emerge, since I have had to make an effort of writing, or re-writing my texts to try and intersect my studies with the general theme of the academic events they were presented at.

**BACK TO
THE THINGS**

The possibility of exploring the relationship between the increasing use of *concretão*,[44] or rough exposed concrete in São Paulo's architecture from the 1950s on and the local concretist art movement, also happening there at approximately the same time, have always intrigued me; but my studies of this subject were not included in the final version of my doctoral dissertation and remained in a drawer, waiting for a better moment to be shown. The 8th Brazilian DOCOMOMO Congress call for papers (Rio de Janeiro, 2009) seemed a good occasion to expound them, even if in an abridged way, as if pointing out to the tip of an iceberg.

At the height of the concretism/neo-concretism art debates, the work of João Baptista Vilanova Artigas transitioned between experimenting with the *carioca* Corbusian language (1946-56) and the brutalist trend (after 1959); between one and other, a certain interregnum can be perceived. Then, two singular houses by Artigas & Carlos Cascaldi were designed, coinciding with the dates of the concretist exhibition – the Baeta House (1956) – and the neo-concretist manifesto and exhibition – the Rubens Mendonça, or Triangles House (1959). These houses follow the formal and composition guidelines that Artigas had been experimenting in his residential works since the mid-1940s, pursuing certain peculiar modes of spatial organization. However, they introduce as a novelty a more blunt and evident use of singularly designed concrete structures, now applied to the domestic scale. Also, both houses seem to dialogue with the artistic, cultural and political debates of the time, especially, but not exclusively concretism.[45]

> What is perhaps of interest to highlight here is that my paper arguments were not developed and presented only textually. At seminars and lectures on architecture oral presentations are usually accompanied by images; but in this case, the images were not mere illustrations of exclusively historical interest, but an intrinsic part of the conception and exposition of the ideas and arguments that were born of a referenced critical recognition of those houses, as seen from the specific angle of their approximation to the concretist art movement. Moreover, I proposed a formal game visually approximating the apparently capricious (but in fact, very rational) hyper-designed columns of both houses by Artigas & Cascaldi and the geometrical manipulations proposed by some concretist paintings. According to the old adage "a picture is worth one thousand words," this approximation allowed me to condense, into a fifteen-minute talk, complex ideas that needed dozens of pages to explain.
>
> My text "Artigas Pop-Cult: considerações sobre a cabana primitiva, a casa pátio e quatro colunas de madeira" starts with an

apparently casual remark: In a late interview Artigas commented that the Berquó House (designed in 1967), would be his *pop* residence. Up to that moment his commentary was exclusively and non-reflexively understood as a reference to the word *popular*. But as I reminded that at the São Paulo Art Biennale of 1967 pop-art was the most present artistic and awarded manifestation, I wanted to verify whether there would be any connection in this case. Of course, Artigas himself helped to shuffle the cards, and he certainly had a lot of fun in doing so: In his commentary he also mentions the wise simplicity of the Baeta's house foreman, and his child's memories of the wooden lambrequins of the State of Parana houses. Anyway, in purely visual, formal and constructive terms, the Berquó House is not quite *popular*. Or perhaps it may be considered as closer to an extremely erudite meaning of the word popular. Better yet, it may be referenced to the *primitive* philosophical current whose origin can be traced to at least the eighteenth century, combined with the typological theme of the patio, not to mention the relationship with pop-art, and possibly other things as well:

The Berquó house, designed in 1967 by João Batista Vilanova Artigas, retakes the ancestral theme of the patio, in this case defined by four wooden trunks which partially support the concrete structure of the house, and which allegorically refer to the paradigm of the primitive hut, understood as a principle and metric of all architecture, as postulated by Laugier and others. To better understand the multiplicity of erudite references of this project we propose a rereading of Artigas' text published in 1969 along with Berquó and Mendes André houses, suggesting a comparison with two patio-houses by José Luis Sert, of a similar formal structure, suggesting the opportunity to understand Artigas' posterior mention to pop, as if referring to the irony of Pop Art as much as to the popular, as a symbol of the original dwelling. It also suggests a reference to the quotidian feminine pragmatism of this house, mentioning along the way other dense complex possible readings. Moreover, these reading peremptorily deny that this or any other of Artigas' works can be reduced to a simplistic approximation between the political situation and the artistic and architectonic creation.[46]

>Longer and more developed than the former, this text also only survives and convinces in the exposition of its argument thanks to the various types of images it contains, aimed to activate references or for comparison to other works, and interpretative drawings by this author concerning the study of proportions and structure.

>In my master's thesis I proposed a reading of Paulo Mendes de Rocha's houses from a chronological, structural and typological

point of view. The set of 42 cases he designed between 1958 and 1995 shows certain design homogeneity, and when they are considered as objects of study they may be deemed as *classical* – in a processual, not stylistic, sense – for his residential works can be read as continuous and constant reworking over some relatively few, clear and well-defined formal and structural guidelines, resulting in each case in new, but always recognizable, variations and combinations. A creative and aesthetic search summed up in the words of master Mies van der Rohe, in a conversation with Philip Johnson: "It is better to be good than to be original."[47]

Some *leftovers* of that thesis such as my studies on the deep shadows ever-present in the majority of the brutalist local houses were presented in a posterior text, "The Shadow Modernity of some Paulista Brutalist Houses,"[48] a kind of phenomenological approach born from what I've learned with my detailed readings during my master's thesis studies that partially complements and partly contradicts it.

The structural organization of some brutalist *paulista* houses based on the use of ribbed and waffled slabs often result in markedly symmetrical constructions, a fact that is sometimes counterpointed by a more informal organization of the non-structural internal partitions. But beyond these material resources, the symmetry is also counterpointed, or diluted, at least from the purely perceptual point of view, by the judicious use of natural and artificial light. To clearly and concisely exemplify this point an *extreme case* was chosen: Mendes da Rocha project for his own house (1964). The structural rhythm and the interior space arrangement had their symmetry shuffled by the apparently capricious, but in fact sufficiently functional, arrangement of the natural zenithal or lateral lightning, corroborated by the arrangement of the artificial lightning devices. The combination of these elements plus the heavy hanging concrete brise-soleil protecting the house two opposite *open* facades – defined

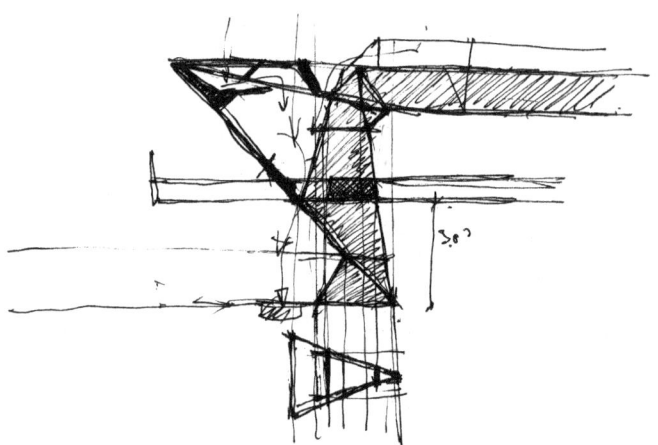

Anhembi Tennis Club, detail of structure, São Paulo SP. Vilanova Artigas and Carlos Cascaldi, 1961. Drawing Ruth Verde Zein

by large linear windows – help avoid direct sunlight entry and provide a *paradoxical* perception of the interior illumination. In this house there is more shadows in the *illuminating* facades and more light in the windowless center, while apparently random spots of natural light organize some special needs of the house functionality. Besides being a sui generis resource for defining the house's interior arrangement, this kind of design strategy, present in this and other São Paulo brutalist works, suggests a deviation from the modern standard pattern of glassed, transparent and excessively luminous boxes, and it does not occur due a lack of *resources*, or because of a *regional* bias, but it is proposed as a creative design solution. And it also suggests the necessity of broaden the definition of what *modernity* is, implying that it would be better to avoid excessively narrowing what may be included in it, as long as we are open to consider the facts from other angles, ours included, to arrive in a more varied, creative and inclusive understading of modern tradition.

But despite its plain detailing and interior penumbra, Mendes da Rocha house does not seek tradition. Neither is it the result of a lack of constructive resources. It displays and purposely seeks a carefully obtained non-illuminated ambiance, partially in contradiction with the fact that it is organized as a tree-like structure. Being an elevated house, it paradoxically does not seek light but shadows and makes an effort to be seen as a closed box; like an artificial cave it has to rely on subterfuges to bring light to some carefully chosen internal places. The rough and matte surfaces and crepuscular interiors reflect another kind of sensibility, tuned to the post-war new building technologies and intensely Manichean political ambiance, with no room for conciliation. As so, they also enrich modern architecture, making it clear that it does not live by light alone.[49]

> None of these close readings or referenced critical recognitions actually explain how to do a critical analysis of a building, and the examples in this text are not included to serve as parameters for other readings, let alone as a partial or complete methodological prescription. They are here more to emphasize the first crucial issue of any reading of a work, which is, what it is for, who is doing it, and why someone decided to do it.

I HAVE TRIED TO CLARIFY, IN GENERAL AND IN EACH CASE, MY CONCERNS AND HOW THEY LED ME TO DO SOME ANALYSIS OR REFERENCED CRITICAL RECOGNITION OF CERTAIN ARCHITECTURE WORKS.

Certainly, my goals and results are a bit clearer for me today because I have dedicated myself to this subject for some time. To those who are starting out along these trails, it would be inane to demand total a priori consistency since that only comes with time; but neither is it wise to leave this demand aside since consistency is only confirmed when the challenge is kept on the horizon.

As much as in the design process, and as any other creative human activity, a critical analysis of an architectural work is always singular, each case is a case; there is neither a recipe nor a method. And yet no human activity, even if creative, can do without both recipes and methods, although provisional and fallible. If we insist, perhaps one day we will arrive at a better understanding of these processes.

I have always disagreed with the statement that "architecture cannot be taught," which only indicates the laziness of the ones that have chosen to be teachers and professors, in the best and broadest sense of the term. Instead, we try.

NOTES

EN. Article previously published at: Ruth Verde Zein, "Há que se ir às coisas: revendo as obras," in: *Leituras em teoria da arquitetura – volume 3: objetos*, eds. Gustavo Rocha-Peixoto, Lais Brostein, Beatriz Santos de

Oliveira and Guilherme Lassance (Rio de Janeiro: Riobooks, 2011), 198-218. Translated by Anita Di Marco and Ann Puntch.

1. "Carta a un joven argentino que estudia filosofía," quoted in: Jose Ortega y Gasset, "Obras Completas, tomo I," *Revista de Occidente*, 1946, 68, http://www.pachami.com/Ensayos/OrtegayGassetylaArgentina.htm#_ftn4.

2. One of the most instigating authors about this theme Richard Foqué, even because he discusses it intelligently and without any immediate subordination to the academic production instruments – opening wider perspectives that would be impossible other ways. In his recent book, Foqué consolidated his studies and proposals on design investigation. Richard Foqué, *Building Knowledge in Architecture* (Antwerp: UPA, 2010).

3. I am speaking of architecture and I suggest that here the term could be understood as a metonymy for the broader field of the creation and transformation of the human environment. But in fact, I am only speaking of architecture, which even so is no small thing.

4. Carlos Eduardo Dias Comas, "Ideologia modernista e ensino de projeto: duas proposições em conflito," in: *Projeto arquitetônico, disciplina em crise, disciplina em renovação*, ed. Carlos Eduardo Dias Comas (São Paulo: Projeto, 1986). Republished in: Ruth Verde Zein, ed., "Projeto como investigação: antologia," *Seminário IV Projetar* (São Paulo: Altermarket, 2009). [CD-ROM]

5. For corroboration, see the quotings below excerpted from: Perez Oyarzun, Alejandro Aravena and José Quintanilla, *Los Hechos de La Arquitectura* (Santiago: ARQ, 2007). Free translation.

6. See Francesco Dal Co, "Criticism and Design," in: *Oppositions Reader*, ed. Michael Hays (New York: Princeton Architectural Press, 1998), 157.

7. Donald A. Schön, *Educando o profissional reflexivo* (Porto Alegre: Artmed, 2000).

8. See chapter: "O Lugar da crítica: nunca é inocente escrever sobre arquitetura," in: Ruth Verde Zein, *O lugar da crítica: ensaios oportunos de arquitetura* (Porto Alegre: Ritter dos Reis, 2002), 201.

9. I'm not losing sight of the fact that architecture is, in the end, only a service that is lent to other human beings who request it and without whom it could not exist. But once requested, how will it be produced? If architectural creative processes were the mere result of outside forces, all architectural proposals under the same conditions (for example, a competition) would be identical, since they are not there is at least this extra *other* that has to be considered and comprehended. Thus, what interests me here is not the efficient cause for the existence of architecture, but its becoming, its process of coming to be, its configuration through creative action.

10. The reverse is also possible: But that is just another thing that will not be treated here, by my free choice, because it is outside my argument.

11. Nicola Abbagnano, *Dicionário de filosofia* (São Paulo: Martins Fontes, 1970), 917, entry "Teoria científica."

12. Marina Waisman, *El Interior de la Historia. Historiografía Arquitectónica para uso de Latinoamericanos* (Bogotá: Escala, 1990, 29). Free translation.

13. Ibid. Free translation. In the original the author refers in this excerpt to Erwin Panofsky, *A perspectiva como forma simbólica* (Lisbon: Edições 70, 1999).

14. Enrico Tedeschi, *Teoria de La Arquitectura* (Buenos Aires: Nueva Vision, 1973). [see the 1962 original edition or the 1972 3rd revised edition]

15. Josep Maria Montaner, *Arquitectura y Crítica en Latinoamérica* (Buenos Aires: Nobuko, 2011), 46. Free translation.

16. Tedeschi, *Teoria de La Arquitectura*, 19. Free translation.

17. Ibid., 20. Free translation.

18. Ibid., 20-21. Free translation.

19. Ignácio Lewkowicz and Pablo Sztulwark, *Arquitectura Plus de Sentido. Notas ad hoc* (Buenos Aires: Kliczkowski, 2001), 50-51.

20. Ibid., 47.

21. Dal Co, "Criticism and Design."

22. Ibid.

23. Peter Eisenman, *Ten Canonical Buildings 1950-2000* (New York: Rizzoli, 2008). This book appears to take up again, in another turn of the screw, his 1963's PhD dissertation: Peter Eisenman, *The Formal Basis of Modern Architecture* (Baden: Lars Muller of Baden, 2006).

24. Oyarzun, Aravena and Quintanilla, *Los Hechos de La Arquitectura*, 20-21.

25. Ibid., 27.

26. T.N.: *Paulista* refers to what or who is natural of São Paulo.

27. Article originally published in: Machado de Assis, "The Ideal of the Critic," *Diário do Rio de Janeiro*, August 10, 1865, São Paulo. And republished in Machado de Assis, *O jornal e o livro* (São Paulo: Penguin/Companhia das Letras, 2011), 8-9.

28. Especially when one wants to study houses: See for example the report made by Cecilia Rodrigues dos Santos and Marlene Milan Acayaba in depositions added to the recent facsimile republication of the classic: Marlene Milan Acayaba, *Residências em São Paulo, 1947-1975* (São Paulo: Romano Guerra, 2011).

29. Ruth Verde Zein, *Arquitetura brasileira, escola paulista e as casas de Paulo Mendes da Rocha* (master thesis, UFRGS, 2000).

30. "Caminhos da Arquitetura" was republished in: João Batista Vilanova Artigas, *Caminhos da Arquitetura* (São Paulo: Livraria Editora Ciências Humanas, 1981).

31. Ibid., 77.

32. As Artigas related in an interview with Aracy Amaral published in: Aracy Amaral, "As posições dos anos 50. Entrevista de Vilanova Artigas a Aracy Amaral," *Projeto* 109, April 1988, 97.

33. As he says in the interview with Lena Coelho dos Santos published in: Lena Coelho Santos, "Fragmentos de um discurso complexo. Depoimento de Vilanova Artigas a Lena Coelho Santos," *Projeto* 109, April 1988, 93.

34. Originally published in: João Batista Vilanova Artigas, "Uma falsa crise," *Acrópole* 319, July 1965. And republished in: Artigas, *Caminhos*, 99.

35. This subject is treated in more detail with appropriate citations in the author's master's thesis: Zein, *Arquitetura brasileira*, especially in Chapter 1.3 "Brutalismo, Escola Paulista: entre o ser e o não-ser".

36. Fernando de Freitas Fuão, "Brutalismo, a última trincheira do movimento moderno," *III Seminário DOCOMOMO Brasil*, São Paulo, 8-11 December, 1999. [oral communication]

37. The critical reading of contemporary architecture has always been a field of my interest since my work as a journalist of architecture and before that, since 1978. But reading the contemporaneous works is a task more related to critique than to theory, and it seemed to me that an academic work in theory, history and critique, the areas of concentration of my master's and doctoral dissertation, required reading works of a certain degree of *historicity*. But both interests are alive in my recent studies.

38. Comas, "Ideologia modernista e ensino de projeto."

39. Ruth Verde Zein, "A arquitetura da escola paulista brutalista 1953-1973" (PhD diss., UFRGS, 2005), http://www.lume.ufrgs.br/handle/10183/5452.

40. Harold Bloom, *A angústia da influência. Uma teoria da poesia* (Rio de Janeiro: Imago, 2002), 23-24.

41. Zein, "A arquitetura da escola paulista brutalista 1953-1973," 73.

42. Ruth Verde Zein, "Concretismo, concretão, neo-concretismo, algumas considerações e duas casas de Artigas," *8º Seminário DOCOMOMO Brasil* (Rio de Janeiro, 2009).

43. Ruth Verde Zein, "Artigas pop-cult: considerações sobre a cabana primitiva, a casa pátio e quatro colunas de madeira," *III Seminário DOCOMOMO Sul* (Porto Alegre, 2010).

44. *Concretão* (big concrete) is the colloquial term used to qualify the brutalist works of the 1950s to 1970s; on the reason and justification for use of the term *brutalist* refer to: Zein, "A arquitetura da escola paulista brutalista 1953-73" or Zein, "Brutalismo, sobre sua definição (ou, de como um rótulo superficial é, por isso mesmo, adequado)," *Arquitextos* 084.00, Vitruvius. May 7 2007, http://www.vitruvius.com.br/revistas/read/arquitextos/07.084/243.

45. Zein, "Concretismo." The citation here had it style slightly corrected, because us authors are always obsessive and dissatisfied, especial with our own texts.

46. Zein, "Artigas pop-cult." Idem for minor adjustments and corrections.

47. Phillip Johnson's comment in his text Philip Johnson, "The Seven Crutches of Modern Architecture," in: *The Architectural Reader. Essential Writings from Vitruvius to the Present*, ed. Krista Sykes (New York: Georges Brazilier, 2007), 171. [original article from 1955]

48. Ruth Verde Zein and Cecilia Rodrigues dos Santos, "The Shadow Modernity of Some Paulista Brutalist Houses," *11º Seminário DOCOMOMO International* (México, 2010).

49. Ibid.

AN ETHICAL PRAGMATIC CRITIQUE, AN OPERATIVE AND REFERENCED THEORY

POSSIBLE AND NECESSARY TOOLS FOR DESIGN EDUCATION

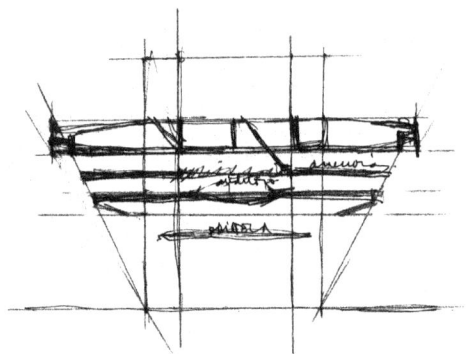

Office of the Municipal Budget of São Paulo, transversal section, São Paulo SP. Plinio Croce, Roberto Aflalo and Giancarlo Gasperini, 1971. Drawing Ruth Verde Zein

Let's start with some *ad hoc* definitions.

Pragmatism can be defined as the belief that a doctrine will be true as long as it is useful and provides some sort of success or satisfaction; besides, a so-called pragmatic point-of-view considers that the concept we may reach about a certain object or situation will be simply the practical outcome derived from the sum of all the concepts that could be conceived around it or that arises from its practical implications. Such definition seems abstract, but it is quite concrete. It is about renouncing any transcendent dimension of concepts; not by denying it (the dimension), but by considering it unattainable in practice. That said, there is only the mere thing itself and all the knowledge originated from that very thing.

Theory can be defined as a corpus or set of knowledge elaborated and structured so as to obtain a certain degree of credibility, and which intends to explain, elucidate, interpret or unify a given domain composed of phenomena or events pertaining to a practical activity. Once again, there is nothing abstract in a theory; nor is it a naive activity. It is not an inconsequential opinion or statement; it can only derive from the deliberate search for order, but it is not necessarily a mere simplification. Thus understood, *theory* emerges from practice: It verifies and analyzes, cautiously researching its nature, aspects, and varieties, going deep in its studies, and it aims to interpret and elucidate.

Moreover, *theory* will always be circumstantial and qualified: It refers to a certain and particular set of topics and interests, and it delimits a specific field within the totality of reality.

On the other hand, a theory is not, nor should it be, a mere summation of somewhat useless information. Its content is not only descriptive, but also interpretative. It aspires to reach a certain amount of consistency and unity, although a complex one. In other words, even when the phenomena or events examined by the will of creating a theory, would be multiple, complex, and even contradictory, theory's mission is to make them intelligible, providing plausible clues to their understanding. Besides, implicitly, a *theory* does not aim to simply understand and interpret, but it also desires to provide, with its reflections, some feedback on the domain it is considering.

And what about *criticism* or *critique*? In its popular sense, as criticism, it is understood as censorship and condemnation, a negative deed. But in its true sense, critique is neutral: It is just the ability to examine and appreciate the works of the human spirit in order to discern, appraise and formulate criteria. It may be linked to morality, that is, to a set of rules of conduct that are considered as valid for a particular and restricted time and place; or it may be linked to ethics, that studies and appreciates the human behavior and qualifies it from the point of view of good and evil, in a relative or in an absolute way. In this sense, a moral criticism would be born from a specific and restricted universe of previously determined *truths*, whereas an ethical criticism would try to understand, assess and qualify human acts and facts; without grounding itself in a priori arguments, but also, without exempting itself from formulating the limits of what is allowable or appropriate.

The basic difference between *theory* and *criticism*, or better *critique*, lies less in the method than in the aims. Both examine and verify data, but while a theory refrains from making moral or ethical judgements and devotes itself to an attempt to systematize the facts it encounters, a critique, as an assessment, does not need nor do not have to arrive at broader conclusions. If it also examines and verifies a fact, it does so to establish value judgments (in a moral criticism), or to test and question intentions, results, and attitudes (in an ethical criticism).

What is *design*? In a strict sense, it means a set of organized ideas and actions to put forward the future execution of an endeavor. In a broader sense, design also means a purpose, or an intention,[1] since it comprises not only the set of tasks needed to materialize something but also the desire to make it real – and it is the desire, as an *unmoved mover*, that initiates the process of planning its realization.

It occurs to me that it would also be necessary to define *history*. I would rather not to do it here, but just try to distinguish *history* from *theory*. For that, I will adopt historian Peter Collins's opinion. In his book *Changing Ideals in Modern Architecture*,[2] Collins states that the crucial difference between history and theory is like the difference between understanding the way buildings were built in the near or remote past, and the way they are built today. Collins admits there is certain danger for contemporary architecture when historians' discourse is too close to architects' daily practice. For him, unlike history, and because it is concerned with the way architecture that is being created today, theory may become a crucial instrument for understanding architects' daily activities.

Collins also refutes the idea that architecture, i.e. architectural forms, are nourished only by other forms in a mere mechanical process. He states that it is the idea that selects which forms should be more appropriately selected that creates the architecture of a certain age. This does not mean that practice comes from theory, quite the contrary: for him, architects "think of forms intuitively, and then try to justify them rationally."[3]

The definitions above are all circumstantial and do not intend to be absolute, they are just pragmatic. They have no other goal than to serve as beacons to begin to formulate some thoughts on the roles of theory and critique in the tutoring/mentoring activities, in architectural design education. They are born from the necessity of reflecting on my personal and limited practice as a professor, and on the accumulation of my experiences as a citizen of these apparently irreconcilable worlds (at least in Brazilian schools of architecture): Theory, history, and design education.

LET'S GO BACK TO THE SUBJECT AND TO THE TITLE

At this point, what could an *ethical pragmatic critique* be? And what about an *operative and referenced theory*? Besides, what does a *theory of architecture* have to do with the process of *architectural design* and, by extension, with the process of *architecture design tutoring*? Before we get there, it is perhaps necessary to present a very brief review of some tendencies present in the architectural, professional and educational panorama in the recent decades, in Brazil, and perhaps around the world.[4]

The lack of a central focus, of a dominant and thus unassailably correct opinion and the openness to the peripheral, to deviations, variations, minorities, and other characteristics of the so-called *post-modern* condition, shook up the world of architecture and architecture education, in most if not all its conspicuously established convictions, causing significant confusion among the unaware, and also, the well aware. With all due respect, and just in order to sum up the situation by drastically reducing it, one may say that the pedagogical attitude in architecture education shifted from the oppressive certainty of enforcing a given model to the difficult exercise of staying put on an aesthetic fence.

As for example: In the 1970s my design professors dismissed critique and theory in their how-to-do because the *right* way to design was considered obvious, and it was just a question of following certain defined steps to grant it. What was taken for granted, and why, are subjects to be described, answered, and discussed on another occasion. What really matters here is that in the 1970s the design domain neglected or dispensed with theory, since someone established *modus operandi* was in force (albeit already worn and leaking like a sieve), which allowed design professors to dismiss the theory and to employ criticism only in a moral sense (of right versus wrong).

Apparently, and according to younger peers' statements, the *battle of styles* finally took place in the 1980s within the architecture programs in Brazil. On the one hand, there were the guardians of the *modern*, and on the other, the supporters of the *post-modern*. The pro-moderns basically invoked tradition to justify its continued validity, a tradition that included the corpus of modern works, but not necessarily the principles the authors had believed or adopted to shape those forms. The so-called post-modernists invoked the need to break with this tradition, which they considered, perhaps too quickly, as exhausted, in order to air out the room. On both sides only a few acolytes were trying to develop any deeper and referenced reflection on the qualities and boundaries of modernism in architecture and its real and concrete (or pragmatic) effects.

In the 1990s (and once again I speak from my own experience, now as a professor), the idea of *style*, as defined by the 19th century academic tradition – as a choice among different possibilities, all of them generically valid, since none could claim to be absolute – was once again stigmatized. Instead, and upside down, it comes back in fashion the idea that architecture comes from *an idea*. This was sometimes called as *neo-modernity*, with some variants such as de-constructivism, minimalism, super-modernism etc., etc., etc. In any case, these *labels* are not, or do not intend to be, *styles*, as they aspired to be elevated as *conceptual options*. But, quite differently from the classical modernity, which they intend to emulate in one octave higher, these conceptual options do not come from certainties of a social and technological nature, conveyed into the architectural realm by the spirit of the new times – as it would have happened in the core of the so-called modern movement. On the contrary, it seemed to be just another type of eclecticism, of a more intricate and deceitful nature, since it was not grounded in an open attitude of appreciation of what was possible and desirable in each case, but after a calculated and aprioristic voluntarism. Starting from any random, fortuitous theme (philosophical, biological, computer-related, quantum physics related, whatever – the more far from architecture, the better), one is allowed to shamelessly affirm to have given birth to some formulas and forms that will certainly assure good architectural deeds, as immediate and miraculous effects of the chosen and extemporaneous corpora of knowledge, quickly enthroned as unescapable truths of authority and consequence – but just for now, because next season everything changes. The debate about the processes of doing became fashionable, in an inherently volatile mood, prone to change according to the next season's swings.

Would this new wave be a reinstatement of the significant role of the theory of architecture?

OR, AS COLLINS EXPLAINS, WOULD THIS BE A RE-VALORIZATION OF THE IDEAS AS THE BASIS OF ARCHITECTURE? NOT AT ALL. IT DOESN'T SEEM SO TO ME – QUITE THE OPPOSITE.

The crucial difference between Collins's definition on the importance of the *ideas* in architecture and this other state of affairs is that now *ideas* are developed and worked out in the abstract, prior to the forms; moreover, the ideas themselves began to gain an ontological value superior to that of the forms. Which is, to say the least, something absolutely foreign to the limited and pragmatic field of architecture practice. It enables architecture as an idea in itself, without any reference to its primary purpose (constructive and tectonic), no longer as a corpus of theory, but as a wild mental speculation – because, let us recollect, theory is not born of disembodied ideas, but of concrete and embodied facts, which a theory analyzes, investigates, and interprets. As for speculation, let anyone who wishes to have fun with it feel free to do so, but as Goya once said, "the sleep of reason produces monsters."

In this scenario, architecture design education remained sit on the proverbial aesthetic fence, but now it became paradoxically allied with the oppressive certainty of enforcing a given model, in a much more perverse synthesis. In brief, anything can be done, as along as an attachment to an *idea* is declared, since it is enough to be a fan of a certain team, or to embrace some unquestionable *truth* to feel secure, and thus stay above all kinds of criticism. Architecture becomes disconnected from its inescapable tradition, and is supported only through a certain *idea*, brought to the arena thanks to some pseudo-relationship that is randomly established with another, non-architectonic, corpus of knowledge, alien, external, unreachable, and brilliant – against which, evidently, the mere pragmatism of architecture as construction will have no influence or control whatsoever.

The basic difficulty in dealing with this clearly distorted situation, which is hugely damaging to the education and to architecture practice, especially in the countries which cannot afford such kind of wasteful and messy experiments, as ours, lies in the fact that we are all totally in agreement on one point only, the refusal of authoritarianism. Thus, we indirectly play the game of confusion, restraining ourselves from trying to curb such a state of affairs for fear of being tagged with the *retrograde* and *authoritarian* label, which we obviously do not want.

Another concern that makes it even more difficult to manage this situation is, surprisingly, to realize how much authoritarianism subtly pervades all the stuff that, for lack of a better word, we can call here as the *quasi-architectures-of-ideas*. Those who espouse this, or that *idea* feel exempt from giving any other satisfaction to the world, from testing their convictions and, even worse, their architectural productions. They are at least enthusiastic neo-converts, and at worst intolerant fanatics; they have no questions at all, just certainties. Since certainties are frequently more comforting than questions, they will not easily yield to the pleas of common sense.

It is quite evident I am exaggerating the general features of the panorama; and I do so intentionally, in order to make it clearer and more obvious. In real life daily struggles, positions are never totally unchangeable or defined, and people navigate very easily (although with no or little coherence) among the most dissimilar attitudes above reported (labeled, to better explain them, as typical of some specific decades). The here and now is always a *mélange* where all these attitudes coexist at the same time, usually in an amorphous way and without too much self-consciousness; which does not help to clarify things at all.

Now. If this panorama is minimally plausible, perhaps the adequate exercise of an ethical and pragmatic critique, and of an operative and referenced theory, could be developed into useable tools, or even indispensable ones, in architectural education. While the critique may be used mostly as an emergency resource, cutting and cauterizing, a correct handling of theory is sure to become indispensable as a medium-term remedy.

I recall that, by the above definitions, both critique and theory are born from the things of reality and do not precede them at all.

The presence of architectural critique in the architecture education should occur only when the design practice has already begun. A minimally responsible architectural critique must refuse to discuss *ideas* which have not yet been put to test on paper or computer screen. The first rule for professors/tutors is to critically discuss only the students' actual products (models, drawings, etc.). This seems to be extremely obvious, but not quite so. There is no architecture critique based merely, for example, on the inputs necessary to begin the design process, such as the brief, location, terrain, and any pieces of architectural repertoire that would occasionally be invoked to reference and support the issue. No matter how refined and detailed these inputs may be, they are not the design, if they have not yet been submitted to some creative elaboration. And here, we do not forget one of the major inputs, the drive and the desire, on the contrary: Architecture can only become a creative elaboration when it is imbued with this ineffable *quid*. However, out of respect for the students, a critique to his/her work can only be ethically committed after and between – after the (two or three dimensional) drawings, and placing a third party between us, the paper or screen with drawings, or the model etc., upon which a critique shall be exercised. Before that, we may talk among ourselves, at will, as is the right of all citizens, but a close reading or a critical tutoring of a design should not be started.

Better to put forward some precisions on the subject of the inputs; they are also apparently obvious but are quite often forgotten. The brief and the location are not immutable data, and the design process will necessarily transform them; they are not absolute, but variables terms of a complex equation. For this reason, the habit of stimulating a first step of exhaustive previous research before the starting of the design process – a common feature in a certain type

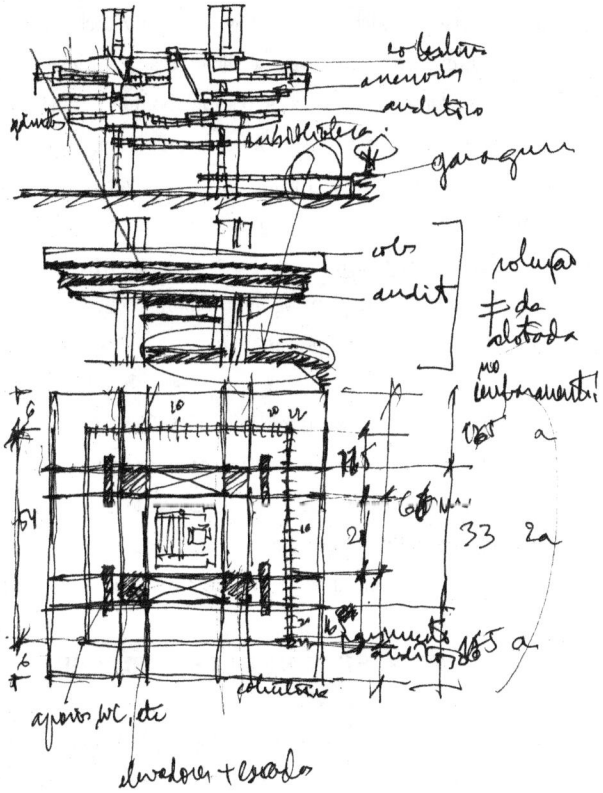

Office of the Municipal Budget of São Paulo, section, elevation and plan, São Paulo SP. Plínio Croce, Roberto Aflalo and Giancarlo Gasperini, 1971. Drawing Ruth Verde Zein

of objectivist approach that is widely common in architectural education – is counterproductive. I would even say that it is probably a mistake to compel the students to know too much about a subject before allowing them to design for two reasons: First, because this attitude evidently inhibits the creation by an excess of undue prior criticism (especially when applied to inexperienced beginners); second, because design itself is a research process, a *reflection-in-action*. It is in the back-and-forth movements among inputs, needs, desires and results of the design process that the students, and architects, start defining the directions in which research needs to be deepened. Trial and error are unavoidable parts of a creative design process; delaying the moment of creation is perhaps a wish to assure an a priori total correctness, *ex cathedra*, as if a creation would be a pure leap and not an intercalation of leap and path, moving away for a while, then slowly, very slowly and laboriously approaching the goal.

LET'S GO BACK TO THE ISSUE OF THE CRITIQUE

The attitude in favor of the introduction of critique as an immediate post-design step could be called *ethical pragmatic critique*. It can be used as an effective design tutoring device. But to get there it requires from professors a vast knowledge of the subject, a knowledge that exceeds and goes beyond their own personal design experience, and includes a wide-ranging overview on the architectonic knowledge field; and, why not, a sort of knowledge that also embodies the basic fundamentals of pedagogical issues. On the other hand, it is important to distinguish the *ethical pragmatic critique* from a *correction*. Correction also has its place in design tutoring, especially in the later stages of the process, or whenever it may occur in a strictly objective way (for example, in an incorrect design dimensioning). But if it goes too far from objectivity, *correction* will in fact constitute an overbearing moral criticism, which simply cannot replace or supersede the value and necessity of an ethical criticism.

The *architecture of ideas* trap is instantly disarmed when one adopts the attitude in favor of an ethical pragmatic critique, precisely due to its pragmatism: The project design will be valued for what it really is, and not for what it intends to be. Intentions and speculations will be then halted. Ethically, one cannot prevent them from occurring, which would neither be possible, nor desirable. Pragmatically, one ignores them, and puts them to the test. In any case, it respects the students' personal creative ability, and even their right to learn by making mistakes.

However, critique in itself, isolated, is not enough to guarantee or promote the quality of architectonic results since it should refrain from giving an opinion, or better, from *inducing*. Then it is up to theory the task of acting in an operative and referenced way, and to serve as an instrument in the process of design tutoring, in order to seek routes to help the development of this elusive category (quality). Theory must so be directly, immediately, and simultaneously invoked (yes, let me be a little repetitive here so that this becomes crystal clear) and superposed to the design process. It is important to consider this issue more closely.

Design professors usually complain that students come too much *unprepared* for the design classes, regardless of whether they are at the beginning, middle or near the end of a program. The complaint has enough foundation, but its solution is never found, since it expects the students to be properly prepared for the *synthesis* of the design process elsewhere, rather than in design classes. Ideally, such preparation would happen through the accumulative knowledge and recognition of a proper architectonic repertoire, with examples from past and recent tradition – modern, contemporary, local, international – as well as through previous and well established technical, technological, dimensional, material and other kinds of knowledge. And traditionally, such knowledge would not be transmitted in design classes, but only in the rest of the curriculum of architecture education programs.

They possibly are, or they are expected to be. But surprisingly, with alarming frequency, when students are faced with the requirements of an architecture design activity, they seem to know nothing, to remember nothing, to have never quite understood anything they might already have studied. And since training and reiteration of such knowledge never seems to be related to design tutoring itself, an apparently insurmountable impasse emerges. But one that may seem unsolvable simply because the question is misplaced.

Perhaps the cause of this stalemate lies in a simple pedagogical reason: The learning process is first of all concrete, and only then abstract, as any elementary school teacher knows. Or, in other terms, and reiterating the initial definitions, theory is always, in law and in fact, post-practice. Thus, as long as the design tutoring process (the practice) does not actively coordinate the learning process of architecture (the theory) and splendidly continues waiting for others to accomplish that task – so that in design classes one will only have the trouble to *practice* the *theory* – this impasse will never be solved.

Once again, I resume the subject of the *operative referenced* theory. Design tutoring is always at least inefficient and at most incompetent when it does not take advantage of the students' works, their designs, as immature as they may be, to theorize. Let's give an example, perhaps in a somewhat simplistic way, but trusting that an example of a *practice* may help clarify my vague *theory*.

Let's take any theme, such as a library (I will decontextualize the issue to clarify the reasoning but note that there is no architecture whatsoever without place, context, urban guidelines etc., but just for the moment let me ignore all that). It seems quite evident to me that it is also the task of design professors to explain, elucidate, interpret and try to put a certain order in the *library* phenomenon, in order to pass on to the students the main generic and basic (possibly typological, in this case) questions of the subject.

Obviously, it is up to the students to research proper examples, although the act of collecting attractive vibrant images from magazines, periodicals, books, and internet portals is no research at all, but simple uncritical amassing. So, I am convinced that it is the design professors' responsibility to demonstrate, in a most pragmatic way, how to go beyond that beautiful collection of clippings and come to a simple, operative, and referenced theory: Operative, because its reach is limited to the issue; referenced, because one can never forget where and why this library is going to be built (and here I contextualize the subject again), which will undoubtedly serve the basis for a selection of viable paths or at least, at first, for the inappropriate or unviable routes.

If an ethical pragmatic critique requires from professors, as stated above, a "vast knowledge of the subject, a knowledge that exceeds and goes beyond their own personal design experience, and includes a wide-ranging overview on the architectonic knowledge field;" an operative and referenced theory requires the same, or even more. To act as design professors, it is adequate to be good architects, it is interesting to be professionals with great practical experience, but it is also essential to be architecture scholars that make an effort to be constantly up to date.[5]

Unfortunately, this last item – that architecture design professors should be scholars in their field of knowledge and not only just active practitioners – does not seem to be much appreciated, valued or even desired in most architecture schools. It is a common claim that in every field there are those who know and those who accomplish, and the latter are preferably chosen to act in architecture design tutoring.[6] This rather fallacious statement leads us to believe that those who practice do not have the knowledge, which is a clearly absurd syllogism; and it also implies that those who do have the knowledge do not practice, which does not have to be an inescapable truth either.

It seems a certain fear of knowledge – or, of *too much knowledge* – remains in the air. It is not a groundless concern, and the vanity of some alleged knowledge-holders contributes to the negative folklore on the topic. However, if there is a wish to change the education of professional architects for the better, it seems undoubtedly necessary to understand and face the effective role of theory and critique in architecture design tutoring.

NOTES

EN. Article previously published at: Ruth Verde Zein, "Uma crítica ética e pragmática, uma teoria operativa e referenciada: possíveis e necessários instrumentos no ensino de projeto de arquitetura," in: *Critica na arquitetura*, eds. Flavio Kiefer, Raquel Rodrigues Lima and Viviane Villas Boas Maglia, (Porto Alegre: Ritter dos Reis, 2001), 289-298; Ruth Verde Zein, "Una crítica etica y pragmatica, una teoria operativa y referenciada, instrumentos posibles y necesarios para la enseñanza del proyecto de arquitectura," *Trim Sessions* 01, 2011, 12-21. Translated by Anita Di Marco and Ann Puntch.

1. In his renowned text "O desenho," an inaugural class delivered at FAU USP in 1967, Vilanova Artigas identifies in the word *drawing* "a remarkable semantic content," because it includes the idea of design as intent. He also states: "no one draws just by the drawing itself." "To build churches, one has to have them in mind, in design." Thus, Artigas sees in the word *drawing* the materialization of the *design*, and more than that he sees in the drawing a device able to help overcome the conflict between art and technique. Although his ideas apparently clashes with the ad hoc definitions used here, it does not seem to me there is a conflict of intentions. In both cases, the drawing continues being valued as an instrument par excellence of architectural thinking and designing, which only comes to life through it. See: João Batista Vilanova Artigas, "O desenho," in: *Caminhos da arquitetura* (São Paulo: Livraria Editora Ciências Humanas, 1981), 39-50.

2. Peter Collins, *Changing Ideals in Modern Architecture 1750-1950* (Montreal: McGill-Queen's University Press, 1978).

3. Ibid., 16.

4. This text was originally written in 2000. A lot has changed since then. Several attempts to resurrect right and indisputable truths have occurred, but luckily, they have mostly failed. The panorama today (2018) remains eclectic, and the considerations here explained are perhaps still valid.

5. Another valuable asset would emerge if professors develop their ability to expound their knowledge in a didactic and proper way. Another apparent truism, but largely forgotten in real life.

6. I want to believe that something has changed in the last twenty years concerning this topic. Or so I hope.

THE SYNTHESIS AS A STARTING POINT AND NOT A FINISH LINE

LET'S START BY REVISING SOME COMMON PLACES: THEY ARE PERSISTENT AND RESILIENT, IF NOT TO CRITICISM AT LEAST TO CHANGES. A REGULAR ARCHITECTURE PROGRAM IS FREQUENTLY ORGANIZED BY PROVIDING SEVERAL ISOLATED COURSES, FREQUENTLY SEPARATED AS EITHER 'THEORETICAL,' 'TECHNICAL' OR 'PRACTICAL.' THE FIRST ONES' MISSION IS TO PROVIDE ACCESS TO A RANGE OF NECESSARILY GENERIC INFORMATION[1] ON THE many facets of architectural knowledge; the later usually includes design studios, where students would exercise the architectural practice (as a sort of simulacrum),[2] to try and accomplish the much-desired synthesis of design, theory and practice in their drawings and in their minds.

How would this process of synthesis occur? Although this is the primary goal of an architectural education, the objective that guides and justifies its program fragmentation, there is only a blurred, unclear and mysterious vision on its feasibility, and no pedagogical clarity at all as how to achieve it. The synthesis is expected almost as a sort of miracle and it is supposed to arrive in some *natural* way. On this subject, we professors maintain a pedagogical passivity that borders on an indulgent fatalism, *washing our hands* and do not taking responsibility for a process that we set in motion, but that will randomly arrive, or not, in the so longed synthesis. And thus, we never propose, nor consider the possibility of inducing or propitiating that synthesis, in a methodical way. The fact that some sort of synthesis does frequently happen, with a reasonable degree of success, considering the precariousness of the process, is an irrefutable proof that God, in addition to being Brazilian,[3] she is also an architect.

The main cause of this absurd situation is, as it has been pointed out and debated in the last two decades,[4] the conflicts between design ideology, didactics and architecture education.

An explanation that, although already widely known, has not been well understood yet, except by a few, and fully ignored by many. Besides, simply naming a problem does not mean it has been overcome.

But, sticking to the subject, it seems to be essential to try and understand how the so-called *synthesis* among *theory, technique*, and *practice* occurs, in architectural education; that is, how these fragmented parts of architectural know-how come together in a concerted way, within the design process. And also, to try and examine some possible ways to promote such synthesis in a pedagogical and responsible way.

So how does this synthesis occur? The first hypothesis to be examined is that it does not, even when the students do manage to propose and develop a design exercise, which may be achieved in a precarious way, without the elaboration of a consistent synthesis of the theoretical and technical information they already have – as it happens every day in design studios. The witty comment among professors is that students have several separate memory sticks, and when leaving a given class, they immediately eject what they have learned and use another blank memory stick in the next class. The same pattern seems to happen at *practical* courses. In the kind of self-standing exercises that are usually proposed in design classes, the bad habit of creating floating, isolated globules of memory is not fought or counterposed, but actively promoted, induced, suggested, reinforced, and expected. No wonder a synthesis does not occur, since when we play the role of design tutors, we do our best to avoid it.

For, in real life, the overwhelming majority of design exercises[5] are usually based on *objective data* that is detached from any practical reality, far from any given context, and with no connection to the immediate or remote tradition of the architectural culture to which we belong. Most often, they are proposed through the displaying of a more or less functionalist use of a brief, configured by diagrams, flow charts, surface charts and the like, and accomplished by the mere drawing of the planar areas needed to attend the program. The outcome of this restrict and pseudo-pragmatic approach will necessarily configure two opposed and antithetical ways, already pointed out by Carlos Eduardo Dias Comas, both dispensing with all and any synthesis with *theoretical* and *technical* knowledge except in a superficial and *a posteriori* way, at best. The first way, objectivist, ignores intuition and creativity and attempts to solve the design problem in an analytical way; the other way, subjectivist, believes only in intuition and creativity and does not intend to solve the problem, but to create a proposition.

**YET AGAIN, ONE WAY FURTIVELY REFERS TO
THE OTHER. THE ANALYTICAL ROUTE WILL
NEVER ARRIVE AT A WHOLESOME SOLUTION, IF
IT HASN'T ALREADY STARTED FROM IT;**

and if it doesn't, it will remain stuck on the road, with too much *utilitas* and very little or no *venustas*. The subjective route, in turn, has the advantage of arriving at a form, perhaps with a certain degree of unity, but the result tend to be too autonomous, with no relationship to context, program, or construction, and will not even become *architecture*, until this haphazard creative process is mercilessly revised, and transformed by tectonic, contextual and objective data.

However, a synthesis could more likely succeed when, as Comas pointed out, the studio[6] has been "transformed into a theoretical-practical activity" that would provide students and professors with "the space and opportunity to study paradigmatic architectonic problems and their solutions." He suggests a few possible topics:

the subject of the peripheric social housing; the community facility next to or in an open public space; a very small house on a plot situated right in the middle of a block; a multifunctional complex; or the re-designing of a downtown urban void.[7]

THE SYNTHESIS AS A STARTING POINT AND NOT A FINISH LINE

Certainly, the definition of sufficiently paradigmatic problems may vary according to place and time, but this proposed scheme is, as I see it, effective enough to make us continue experimenting with it, perhaps even exchanging experiences on how to do it better.[8]

However, even if it is possible (and something similar has already been proposed) to review the design courses to avoid the functionalist-subjectivist double bias and to introduce theory into design tutoring, the common tripartite structure that regulates most architectural education programs is still there, so the need to promote a synthesis of the practical and theoretical knowledge that is provided in each different course has not yet been deciphered, just ignored. This problem would be irrelevant if the practical-theoretical studio would be able to accommodate the *entire* program, in spite of the previously existing fragmented structure, which would remain untouched, but annulled. Apparently, this could be a solution: To discard the tripartite division of theory/technique/practice for the return (because historically we came from there) to the supreme studio, advocated by its masters. It would be perfect, except by a most relevant issue – something that the so tempting but excessive primacy of the studio may have us believe as being of less importance, when in fact it is crucial.

Universities, and inside them, architecture programs, do not exist only to *train* students to know how to respond to certain concrete, even if paradigmatic, demands (i.e., with certain degree

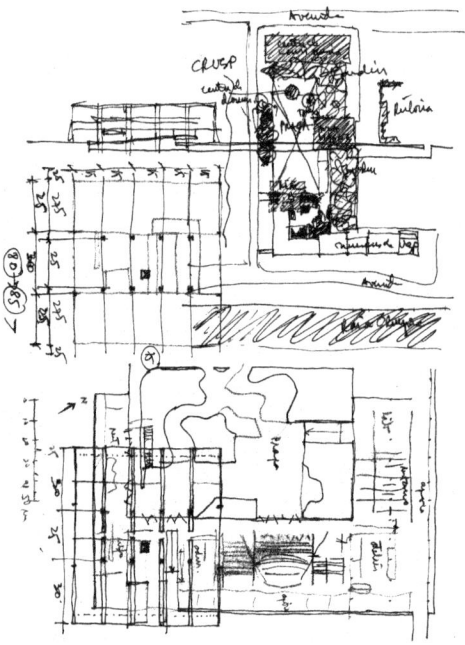

Museum of Contemporary Art of USP, transversal section, master plan, structural scheme and first floor plan, São Paulo SP. Paulo Mendes da Rocha, 1975. Drawing Ruth Verde Zein

of generality), but also and, as important as that, to prepare them to produce fresh knowledge, either by answering to non-paradigmatic cases and unexpected situations, or by exercising their creativity in the wider domains of architecture as a discipline which although has always been and will always be centered on design, is absolutely not limited to it.

To put it in a simple brief manner, not everything can or should be learned in the studio, even in its theoretical-practical version. Here we understand the studio as that place where, par excellence, people should seek and necessarily find proper, finite, specific, and referenced solutions for concrete, limited and specific problems, even when they are potentially paradigmatic, posed as questions that the design aims to answer. The production of architectural knowledge is, and will always be, deeply related to design; but it is not always necessary to propose an unequivocal design solution[9] every time one needs to understand, recognize, and characterize architectonic issues in general.

Consequently, in addition to proposing that the design studio be transformed into a theoretical-practical discipline, it is also urgent to propose that *theoretical* and *technical* disciplines be increasingly transformed into theoretical-practical activities, as well.[10]

I am not avoiding the issue, just observing its real and complex dimensions, that have nothing to do with the fragmentation of courses, we are obliged to admit, for one reason or another. Even if this fragmented structure exists, and has to be maintained, that does not mean it is correct from a pedagogical point of view. The illusion that results from structures organized in fragmented, hierarchized, and bureaucratic ways, as it happens in architecture education, is to make us believe that they are if not everlasting, at least indispensable – not in real life where perhaps they are, but as categories of thought, which they are not. While we keep discussing design tutoring separately from theory, history and technical subjects as if they were truly watertight isolated issues, giving them different values and importance; and while we wait for the best, that a synthesis of this forced fragmentation will occur, as an extra dose of grace, we will be perpetuating the worst of an almost inevitable evil, which is, the bureaucratic institutionalization of this tripartite division. Since it exists and has deeply rooted problems, one could try and use it a more proper way, at least until something better comes along to replace it.[11]

After discarding the academic solution of a practical-theoretical studio as a substitute for the *entire* architecture program and guaranteeing the need for the so-called theoretical/technical disciplines to be transformed into *theoretical* and *practical disciplines*, maybe all this together will lead us to a better promotion of a *synthesis*. It will certainly be a betterment, but perhaps it won't be enough:

THE SYNTHESIS AS A STARTING POINT AND NOT A FINISH LINE

A residue of fragmentation will still exist, and the synthesis is still not guaranteed, but it remains as a messianic expectation.

Perhaps there is a simple solution to ensure that the desired *synthesis* will occur in a full and responsible way; but its simplicity is much more complicated than one might presume. Perhaps it would be enough to imagine that the synthesis is not to occur elsewhere (in another place and in another time) but today, here and now, whichever course we are teaching, for any bureaucratic, practical or customary reasons. The synthesis is not to appear after, but before: One does not arrive there, but starts from there – or else it will never happen. In very simple terms (but whose practical feasibility will always be highly complex), the synthesis is to be there while each student, or professor, at each moment – in the studio, in the lecture room, in the laboratory – fight against the specificity of the knowledge they are supposed to transmit or receive, in order that any knowledge is always, at any moment, permeated by the *synthesis*.

Learning is at first an imitative art, until someone acquires via practice a complete mastery of his/her artistic ability. Learning always involves an external, rhythmic and repeated effort before it is completely assimilated by the persons who experience such (we hope) beneficial influence. The pedagogical agents of education – we, professors –, should constantly seek the best way to enlighten students and to make them realize that all architecture is always there, contained in every issue, however small and specific it looks like. And nothing less than this.

NOTES

EN. Article previously published at: Ruth Verde Zein, "A síntese como ponto de partida e não de chegada," in: *Projetar. Desafios e conquistas da pesquisa e do ensino de projeto*, eds. Fernando Luiz Lara and Sonia Marques (Rio de Janeiro: EVC Editora Virtual Científica, 2003), 81-84; Ruth Verde Zein, "La Sistesis no es el Punto de Llegada sino el de Partida," *Trim Sessions* 01, 2011, 22-37. Translated by Anita Di Marco and Ann Puntch.

1. That is, immediately useless or not employable, despite being eventually prone to provide some practical benchmarks, probably also useless, but of alleged objectivity.

2. By *practice* one might imagine that students would really build something, experimentally or not, or to work directly serving a community (of non-architects, i.e., the general public) so as to *practice* their trade, overseen by mature professionals. With rare exceptions, such activities never occur in our schools' curricula, and we are always inventing either pragmatic excuses or ethical justifications never to put these possibilities into practice. We are the sole professional occupation that does not train our young professionals before throwing them into the labor market and we find this normal and correct. There is something very wrong in all this, but we never really get to know what it is, do we?

3. T.N.: There is an old saying in Brazil claiming God's nationality, considering the countries natural beauties. Here it is used as a double twisted irony, one that has recently been deepened by tragic tones.

4. An indispensable reference on the subject of design education is the book by Carlos Eduardo Dias Comas, ed., *Projeto arquitetônico disciplina em crise, disciplina em renovação* (São Paulo: Projeto, 1986) – in free translation, the title would be: architectonic design, discipline in crisis, discipline in renovation –, with texts by Jorge Czajkowski, Elvan Silva, Carlos Eduardo Comas, Rogério de Castro Oliveira, Edson da Cunha Mahfuz and Alfonso Corona-Martinez. When I reread it, before writing this text, I almost opted to simply just quote it, instead of writing something new, since it seems to me that everything is already there, and that nothing that is criticized or elucidated in that book has been reasonably understood already, nor its suggestions effectively implemented. There is among architects a questionable tendency as to discard invaluable contributions just because they have aged a few years, even when they remain up-to-date. It is a bad habit, like other bad habits of which I speak of in this text. Thus, the present work does not intend to ignore or overcome this primordial effort, but only to give it a modest continuity.

5. It hits my mind that this is an unsubstantiated statement, since I had not accomplished any extensive survey as how design classes are performed, in several schools, in different parts of Brazil, let alone in the rest of the world. But I really doubt that this is a frivolous statement, because it is born from a critic observation of decades of personal experiences as an architect and a design professor, stimulated by the brotherly exchange of information with my peers from other parts of my country and elsewhere. But of course, this is not scientifically proven. Perhaps these and other obvious statements should be someday properly parameterized.

6. *Studio*: A mythical space where, legend has it, architecture students design; a kind of cross between a primordial Eden, the Bermuda Triangle and black holes; today, in transition, between a drawing square and a mouse.

7. Comas, *Projeto arquitetônico*, 43.

8. As for example it happened in the Projetar Seminars that are being held since its first edition in 2003, when this text was originally presented.

9. For example, it is quite common to hear and observe some architects – and some talented students – refuse to understand the topics pointed out by some works of architecture of this or that author, when they do not like that work in terms of aesthetic affiliation, something that becomes crystal clear when they declare: "I wouldn't do it like this", in an *a priori* denial gesture. Nonetheless, in an architecture tutoring that intends to be critic, ample and well-grounded, this is an absolutely irrelevant reaction, at worst, a narrow-minded one. After all, you don't have to share an idea to better understand it and, on occasions, to explore the concepts contained by these and other possibilities. A proper architectural education admits, as a sine-qua-non contemporary condition, the idea of tolerance and plurality. Contrary to what biased people fear, you don't have to be afraid of the moments of aesthetic indefiniteness during the design process; You'd rather use them as a quest to better understand and qualify the problem at hand. A huge amount of ignorance disguised as arrogance, and an excessive haste to delimit one's own field of human and architectonic interests, won't lead to convictions but to dogmatism. These banal – though not rare at all – example shows quite clearly what I mean when I say that architecture education cannot be solely linked to the design process moments, when students should give a responsible and unequivocal answer to a complex question. It should be fomented also in situations in which they won't inevitably have to discern and choose. While you still don't have clearly understood your own ideas, a certain *suspension of judgment* is a good attitude in any learning process – although it will be inescapably overcome when the proposing moment arrives.

10. I will not specify here how this could be done, because I am sure that this is more a matter of recognizing other experiences that are already under way, in many schools and by many peers, than want to try and invent a generic and ingenious *ex cathedra* solution.

11. It is really disappointing, but I do not have some magical answer to replace this tripartite structure for a more perfect and ingenious one. In the meantime, pragmatically, as an architect, I will not sit still and wait for the ideal plot, the ideal client or the ideal budget, but I will accept to work with what I have and try to make the best of any situation. If, by chance, any enlightened colleague has a better solution, I am always ready to adopt it, after ruthlessly examine it.

BR　　LATIN AMERICA:　　　　CRITICAL
5　　　THOUGHTS　　　　　　 READINGS

WHEN DOCUMENTING IS NOT ENOUGH

BUILDINGS, DATES, REFLECTIONS, AND THEORETICAL CONSTRUCTIONS

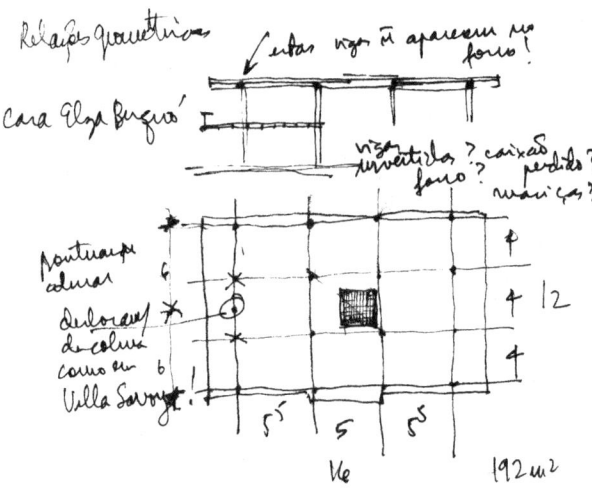

Elza Berquó Residence, longitudinal section and structural scheme, São Paulo SP. Vilanova Artigas, 1967. Drawing Ruth Verde Zein

It is important to respect the documents. But documents do not speak for themselves: They expect to be interpreted. It is never too late to remember, as pointed out by Marina Waisman, that

although the objects of reflection come from reality, the problems they entail are not revealed in a direct or evident way: It is through reflection that the questions underlying the factual reality will be discovered or revealed; the act of questioning is based on concepts and ideas and discoveries are made based on these concepts; afterwards, the praxis will respond – positively or negatively – to the questions or demands formulated by the reflections.[1]

Documents, including works of architecture – which are documents of the highest importance and density in our field of study –, wait patiently for our considerations. But their interpretation will never be exhausted: At any moment, a new look may infuse them with a new life. The same documents, illuminated by other questions, will suggest other precisions and revisions, from prosaic to groundbreaking ones. Yet, for this to happen, new questions must be allowed to emerge. Without systematic questioning there is no expansion or revision of any field of knowledge. And it will only consistently occur as long as we accept that not everything is sufficiently clear, said or defined;

and to change that, we have to make an effort to go back to the origins – the documents – and reexamine them.

As for example. Apparently, there is an underlying dominant idea that pervades almost every canonical historiography of modern architecture, particularly those that deal with other non-European modernity. It is a subtle and hard to detect idea, because it rests at the base and supports many others, so it is taken for granted and rarely discussed because it is seen as a given. I am talking about the notion of *cultural transposition* – of ideas, models, forms etc. According to this notion our (the other's...) architecture came into being by following an imaginary axis originated in the North and reverberating in the South. From the moment one accepts this idea, an implicit corollary immediately takes place: The notion that architectural facts, works, discourses, tendencies, and discussions take place first and necessarily up there and only then down here. After establishing this corollary, and to confirm it, explanations are construed, real or supposed, about how and why this is the way it is; and finally, people validate these explanations by adopting the belief that such basic idea would in fact be the efficient and necessary cause for the things to be as they are (in such an airtight vicious circle that no one notices it).

After things are put like this, so they remain – the law of inertia makes them motionless until something/someone pushes them vigorously. However, it may occur, for example, that a certain researcher – a less informed person, not so much on his/her knowledge of works and documents, but on the constraints of how one *had better* think (that is, what is considered acceptable to think) – decides to examine the facts, the documents, all over again: The tangible architecture buildings, their design and construction dates, and their peculiar traits.

Let us say, hypothetically, that this researcher realizes that all the works of architecture that could be called modern[2] appear basically at the same time, either in the North or in the South, popping up within a temporal range of less than a decade and, in many cases, at very close dates. This researcher might even find out that some of the Southern examples, said to be modern, have even earlier design and completion dates than those of the alleged Northern pioneers. Eventually, this scholar might even discover such a significant number of such *exceptions* that, with these data in hand, she/he feels entitled to start doubting that things have happened the way canonical historiographies affirm, and that perhaps it would be the case to revise them.

However, this hypothetical researcher will very quickly find out that it is hard, really hard to convince her/his peers that what she/he has in hand is nothing other than a bunch of anomalies. Our researcher's work will be doubted, people will accuse her/him of misinterpretation or error, and if that is not enough, she/he will be called names – nationalist, regionalist, feminist, chauvinist etc. This scholar's questions, doubts, facts and diverse theoretical constructions will be disregarded, for things "are not supposed to have happened the way they did," because they are allegedly prevented from doing so, for the sake of maintaining the prevailing theoretical framework, where they have already being put to rest inside (or ignored by) canonical constructions, which were born from some limited chosen facts, but whose universal validity is granted by extension, by customary habits, and by laziness.

Surely, we are talking about a hypothetical case: Nothing of the sort has ever occurred among us – has it? – especially if we are dealing with the works of architecture from the so-called first modernity, from 1920 to 1945. But sorry, I am sure it did happen, and it still does. Several authors have already experienced similar situations and addressed this subject, many times. But their contributions, even when reluctantly accepted, will tend to be tagged, at the best, as episodic events, as some sort of distortion, as minor and less significant cases when considering a wider frame (and many other excuses of the sort). Even the accumulation of such type of studies does not seem to be enough to easily break through this barrier. Perhaps these *other* cases are really anomalies – but perhaps they are not. Anyway, documentation on its own is not enough to demonstrate the argument that something needs to be revised: It is also necessary to be allowed to propose new questions and to establish new reflections in order to question the theoretical constructions that are already in force.

THE ISSUE GETS MORE TENSE WHEN IT COMES TO INTERPRETING THE FACTS OF MODERN ARCHITECTURE OF THE SUBSEQUENT DECADES, NAMELY, THE 1945-75 PERIOD.[3]

Despite the change of context and decades, the idea of cultural transposition – which surely has its value in the process of understanding, analyzing and studying the moment of the so-called first modernity – rests ingrained in the theoretical frame of analysis in such a way, that the historiographic studies addressing the mid-20th century architecture keep on using it. Somehow this interpretation gets crystalized and remains comfortably installed, and thus it is adopted, far and wide, per se and without further examination, in architectural historiographies, to explain the facts happening from then on. This truism is maintained not so much because new facts call it to the stage, but quite often just by inertia. It keeps on being adopted not thanks to a profound and well-grounded analysis of the facts; indeed, should the facts be deeply examined, they would actually preclude its use. The *cultural transposition* idea (or a plain unidimensional version of this complex idea) is automatically adopted because it has become a gadget, a tool, a second-degree prevalent idea: An a priori.

For all that, several researchers do persist in using that already mentioned imaginary axis, flowing from up there towards down here, as the ground basis for their interpretation of the post-1945 architecture works, mechanically believing in it is existence and guidance, in its usefulness to interpret the so-called second modernity. The idea of cultural transposition, extracted from the time boundaries in which it perhaps had some degree of pertinence (at most, before the Second World War), is made to survive beyond its creation and expiration dates. It overflows, assuming a role that is not its own: That of a canonical and unquestionable instrument, that goes on being invoked just because, even when its prevalence and usefulness appear to be less and less defensible and more and more undue; as so, it is applied from top to bottom, over the modernity of other decades, and of other places.

Let's imagine that our hypothetical and nosy researcher comes back to the scene and begins to notice, based on facts – on well-grounded study of the documents, projects, works, their design and construction dates, and the buildings' characteristics

– considering some pieces of architecture designed and built in the 1945-75 period. Let's say that the documents, and mainly their design dates do not suggest the admittance of any a priori *cultural transposition*, let alone the prevalence of the cardinal point North of the imaginary axis, on the South. There can be, and there are, influences,[4] but in such a way that suggests the existence of a complex net, a web, a cloud – but not a one-way axis.

Regardless, it is still going to be hard – really hard – to make this hypothetical researcher's peers consider that there might be something rotten in the simplistic *transposing* view used as an universally valid explanation to what happens in the states to the South of Denmark, in the post-1945 modernity, too. For sure, this is just a hypothetical researcher – but considering everything that has been studied and published, in Brazil and elsewhere, on the subject, neither you nor I can in good conscience believe that any more. And yet *eppur non si muove*.[5]

Another example. For many good reasons, the 1920-45 period is recognized as defining the initial moment of 20th century architectural modernity. This statement, even if it is widely accepted and applied, was not originated spontaneously: It was born from a circumscribed situation, and right or wrong, it was deduced by the consideration of some modern buildings – but not from all of them. However, the historians who support this statement usually do not hesitate to immediately universalize it, due to the king's navel syndrome (which dictates that a citizen of a place believed to be central tends to accept that what she/he thinks is automatically shared by the entire universe).

From this definition another collateral corollary emerges: Everything that happens after 1945 will be per force considered as a secondary development of the first modernity moment, more of the same, a consolidation of a clear, defined, established and fully accepted agenda. And if by chance, some of the architectonic facts happening in this second moment cannot be clearly included in this sort of *continuity* (as a deducted from the reexamination of documents), the solution to explain this apparent oxymoron is to consider these other facts under a minus sign: As a distortion, a misrepresentation, a deviation and a loss of a *true* meaning; the

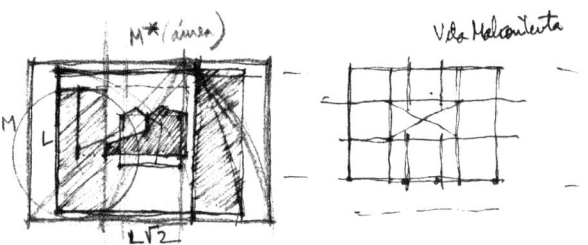

Elza Berquó Residence, scheme of the plan composition,
São Paulo SP. Vilanova Artigas, 1967. Drawing Ruth Verde Zein

latter, of course, being the original, the once and for all founded and established truth about modernity – which of course pertains to another place and time, which is not here, among us, the *others* (nor could it be, due to the prevalence of the previous axioms).

Well then: Our unwary, hypothetical, and nosy researcher comes back to the stage and decides to ask, think and demonstrate – based on the available documentation – that some other interpretations seem to be much more reasonable and in line with the facts, opening up other possibilities of interpretation of the phenomena at hand.

Once again, it will be quite difficult for this researcher's peers to accept what she/he has to say, or for them to fully understand the full extensive nature of the alternative interpretations proposed by this *other* scholar. Bare facts are not enough to convince anyone:

THE HISTORIOGRAPHICAL THEORIES AND INTERPRETATIONS THAT REGULATE THE FIELD WILL REMAIN UNDAUNTED AND WILL NOT BE EASILY BENT BY ANY 'NEW' FACTS THAT MAY JEOPARDIZE THEIR VALIDITY.[6]

Well, not quite the theories themselves, but the field they tend to conform and delimit, the arenas where they reverberate and through which they affect all the other stances. New interpretations based on the reexamination of documents – which may be considered as innocent actions – may eventually cause important conceptual cracks. They might be absorbed by the field, like small waves, without much ado, until the moment they accumulate so much that the people begin to admit that this is undeniably an earthquake, or something much bigger; and, consequently, much more challenging and difficult to bear.

And thus, modern architectures situated in *other* geographical areas, which have been historically established in the *after* decades, keep on being read and interpreted, always and necessarily, as delayed accomplishments, as the result of influences coming from above, in a one-way manner, from there to here, as subsequent and secondary – even when they are not. Probably the first axiom will be applied to them: They will be considered (because they are elsewhere and afterwards) facts necessarily born of some sort of one-way *cultural transposition*. As said before, it is a vicious circle, and those who are down here, in this other cardinal point, will always be the losers.

Fortunately, we live in the 21st century, an era when variety and complexity are both viable and admissible. We started valuing openness to other possible approaches. We live and accept plurality; we are allowed to expand and vary.

Yet in most cases opening and varying does not necessarily mean questioning. They may just wish to politely add or contribute, without jeopardizing the status quo. Other points-of-view are allowed, of course, if and when they are superficial and sketchy. Other subjects and matters may also be considered, as long as they do not provoke any significant disruption. Well-behaved diversity is allowed, and moreover, it relishes on its secondary position because it aspires to be accepted by the current hierarchy that magnanimously includes it, just for the sake of political correctness. It is welcomed because it invigorates the arena with new topics and subjects and suggests that the field is free, just because it is being enriched with new cultural-geographical views. Diversity is accepted as long as it does not confront, in any harsh way, whatever has been set, rests in peace, and is supposedly well established. Yes, we can, we are allowed to – as long as we agree to find our own place, preferably on the fringe, never questioning the very core of the current foundational truths (or myths), enforced in a way that makes everyone forget that these were and are only half-truths; and of current theories, which by inertia and abuse of authority had their validity perpetuated *ad nauseam*.

Actually, expanding the field should be much more than just the indulgent act of allowing *others* to have their *peripheral place*. It is, perhaps dangerously, to call into question the very existence of a core, from which the polarities emanate and from where they are supposedly commanded, before, now and forever. And perhaps the question is not to replace one center for another, but simply to admit plurality in a less biased and much broader way.

These considerations would be just some exercises over nothing if not for the fact that although they are represented here as abstractions, in fact they were born from very concrete situations. They are reflections based on something apparently basic and innocuous – documents – and the realization of their potential to transform the field whenever one looks at them and raises new questions, without merely accepting ready-made ideas, that should be reasonably filtered and validated before being adopted. (New) Ideas may be born of the careful and precise verification of some of our denser documents: The designs and the built works; and of the careful and precise verification of their dates. It seems little, but it is not.

As long as a research is limited to verifying facts, it may look harmless. But when she/he analyzes and compares documents, including buildings, situated anywhere in the world, and considers them, in principle, on equal footing – i.e., just as documents, without the filters of any a priori ideological and/or historiographical explanations –, a research may end up verifying and establishing some very distinct conclusions than the ones that were previously in force. It might happen – as it does – that these results render unfeasible the idea of a simplistic *cultural transposition*, along with other a priori tools, that usually tend to cloud one's vision and to prevent the researchers, who study documents, from finding anything other than the confirmation of the same, the old, the polarity of backwardness etc. But if we allow ourselves to overcome these ideological barriers, other hindrances fall more easily. Documents, when properly examined, according to their own nature and characteristics, not only validate but also strongly suggest different ways to look at them.

Although the above considerations were born from the study of documents – designs and built works, their dates and characteristics –; and although they may suggest clear and honest (other) conclusions, they may end up being affected by the existing bias and habits of the field; and therefore, they may be received, even by the researcher itself, with a certain amount of incredulity. The interpretations they suggest, and their full consequences, may be difficult to understand and admit, especially when a researcher's mind-set is stuck into prevailing theoretical constructions, without quite noticing that the latter have just become anachronistic.

The same facts – the documents – when observed from other angles, can give way to other assumptions and distinct consequences and may display some potential to undermine, even if partially, what seems to be quite well-established. Perhaps that is the reason why new (and apparently outrageous) interpretations, even then they were born from careful reflection over documentation, have such a difficult time in achieving credibility. It is not because they are unreasonable, but because they are overcast by the previously accepted theoretical constructions that are surreptitiously hindering the field.

SOME FINAL REMARKS

The content of this article was born from a critical reflection upon concrete personal experiences – here presented in a somewhat sarcastic mood. My studies on the brutalist works of the 1950s to the 1970s began in the 1980s and were consolidated in my master thesis and doctoral dissertation (1995-2005). They initially considered São Paulo's examples, then other works throughout Brazil, and then examples from several parts of the American continent, and beyond, were included. They have always been supported by the documents: The buildings, their dates, their comparison, and they always thrived without uncritically or naively accepting the existing *canonical explanations* (that I am fully aware of, as I should), at least not before submitting these established assumptions to the test of the concrete information that was being collected.

The amount of information thus gathered prompted the need to deliver a historiographical revision of *brutalism*, as a historiographical (and stylistic) category. The research is still in process (as any ever-ending research); but some very clear premises and results will be briefly mentioned bellow.

As it happens, when my studies are communicated in essays, symposiums, lectures and, especially, when they are presented to my peers – to those who believe they know much more by reading the classics, and to those who have never thought about the subject but do have opinions about it –, these studies tend to be received with an attitude of incredulity. Not that my peers question the facts I present, as they never bother to reexamine them at all, as to determine whether my hypotheses and conclusions are valid. My studies and ensuing findings and theoretical hypotheses are doubted mostly because they contradict the *authorities*, which of course, are not from here, but from abroad.[7] The fading memory of *canonical* texts that were read during the infancy of our education as architects seem to have greater precedence and more authority than a contemporary, systematic, careful and well-grounded research, whose results cast doubt on those previous texts by demonstrating their weaknesses and shortcomings. What seems to be in question is the granting of authority that is bestowed upon, or not, to people – rather than to their studies and research, as it should be.

Yet I fear that in due time the interpretations I have been suggesting, now for decades, will become canonical themselves, but not for good reasons: Just because I so often repeat them, or because others start repeating them, they might end up being accepted, and

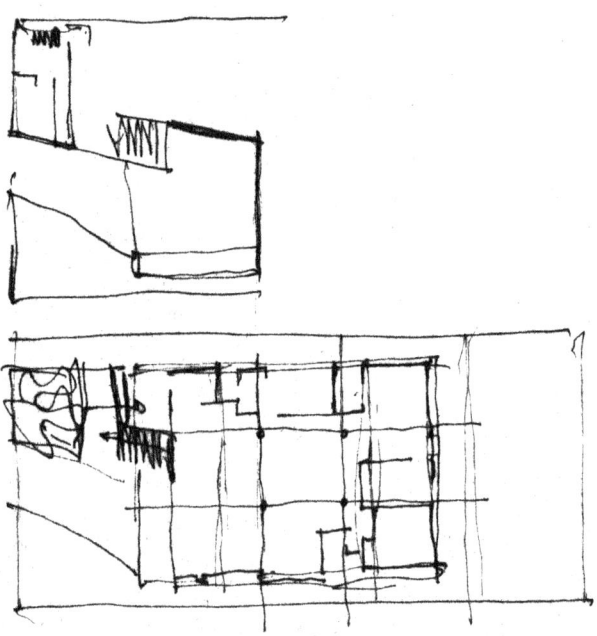

Elza Berquó Residence, ground floor and first floor plans,
São Paulo SP. Vilanova Artigas, 1967. Drawing Ruth Verde Zein

they will gain authority without any accurate critical examination of their content. They may change its status from subversive to obvious, without having passed by the intermediate phase of a careful examination, by my peers, of their assumptions. This said, I would like to make clear that my goal is not to convince anyone except by force of the facts themselves. In other words, by the interpretation of the documents, and not by any ideological or customary way. Likewise, I hope my work would be critically evaluated, and not summarily judged by any a priori antipathy.

Anyway, I will insist and reassert, here again, the conclusions of established and in-progress studies on the so-called brutalism[8] of the 1950s-70s. As far as I go, geographically speaking, some of these hypotheses keep on making perfect sense, albeit they were originally drawn for São Paulo case studies, which confirms my hypotheses that brutalism is not a local phenomenon, but a universal one.

They point out that brutalism was a very prevalent architectonic trend worldwide in the 1950s-70s, configuring another kind of *international style* of that period, since the label may be applied to a wide variety of works designed by almost every living architect in practice during those decades; that this *style* has always been disliked, and even execrated by critics and historians right after its consolidation, expansion and decline, a condition that helped to write off and forget all those works for several decades, both the bad and the good ones (of which there are many); that its contribution is still alive through the traces it has imprinted on the education of many younger architects who are in the practice today, and can be observed as being ingrained in some current architectonic trends in contemporary design practice. Because it is somehow still alive, we had better carry out the historiographic recovery of brutalism and its most important and best works, either to qualify or, perhaps, even to overcome its hidden presence in the contemporary design panorama. To recover its status, or better, to grant it a renewed status, it is important to admit that brutalism is something less than a style, but that it tended to become one; that it was probably not a *movement*, as it lacked self-referenced discourses; that it was configured and established nearly simultaneously at almost everywhere in time and in space; that the facts and dates of works that may be, from a contemporary point of view, be labeled as brutalist, indicate that it did not originate in Britain, nor was necessarily or predominantly influenced by the British case – which undoubtedly is an important case, as are other cases, but neither dates nor traits enforce the interpretation of being *the original* source of the matter. And that, obviously, brutalism has nothing to do with some sort of effigy of Nordic gods on coins.

It was a wide universal phenomenon that included local variations of great interest, and even though it has occurred simultaneously everywhere in the world, which makes it impossible to detect a predominant central origin, it surely owes a debt to Le Corbusier's remarkable contributions and, secondarily also to Mies van der Rohe and other creators; that it might have occurred earlier and more vigorously and inventively in the countries that used to be labeled as of the *third world*; that it is not an ethics but an esthetics, even admitting that most often the designers seemed to prioritize a certain operational ethics that sought to highlight the structural features of a building, and a restrict palette of materials, that it does not have an essence, since what all brutalist works have in common is their surfaces. It still remains as a cursed, taboo, and provocative subject – and therefore, it is still a most interesting one.[9]

NOTES

EN. Article previously published at: Ruth Verde Zein, "Quando documentar não é suficiente: obras, datas, reflexões e construções teóricas." *Anais do 9ª Seminário DOCOMOMO Brasil* (Brasilia: FAU UnB, 2011); Zein, "Quando documentar não é suficiente: obras, datas, reflexões e construções teóricas," *ArchDaily Brasil*, 02 dez. 2012, www.archdaily.com.br/84215/quando-documentar-nao-e-suficiente-obras-datas-reflexoes-econstrucoes-teoricas-slash-ruth-verde-zein; Zein, "Cuando documentar no es suficiente: obras, fechas, reflexiones y construcciones teóricas," in: Maria Dolores Muñoz, Maximiliano Atria, Leonel Pérez and Horacio Torrent, eds., *Trayectorias de la Ciudad Moderna* (Concepción: Universidad de Concepción, 2012), 22-28. Translated by Anita Di Marco and Ann Puntch.

1. Marina Waisman, *El Interior de la Historia. Historiografía Arquitectónica para Uso de Latinoamericanos* (Bogotá: Escala, 1990), 35. Free translation.

2. This is neither the place nor the time to discuss how to validate the appreciation of the term *modern*. Not because it lacks in importance, but not to get out of the focus on this text subject. However, its definition is neither peaceful nor simple, and craved with ideological and geographical bias that would need to be expounded. But I need to discuss some pressing matters before discussing the *modern* classification, which will be proposed in another moment. I share the doubts displayed by Goldhagen concerning a purely stylistic classification of modernity; but in my case, I do not wish to abolishing the parameters of style and shape to consider a definition of modernity, although I acquiesce that they don't need to be the sole judgment parameters. And also because for us – the others – what does interest is to open the field, but not to hastily validate new ideological barriers that would eventually prevent us from entering the same field. See: Sarah Williams Goldhagen, "Something to Talk about: Modernism, Discourse, Style." *Journal of the Society of Architectural Historians* 64/2 (June 2005): 144-167 <www.jstor.org/stable/25068142>.

3. Neither is this the moment to discuss why the panorama changes radically after 1945, and in any case the subject is addressed by many different authors, even implicitly – such as in Josep Maria Montaner, *Después del Movimiento Moderno* (Barcelona: Gustavo Gili, 1993); or explicitly as in Maria Alice Junqueira Bastos and Ruth Verde Zein, *Brasil: arquiteturas após 1950* (São Paulo: Perspectiva, 2010).

4. The author uses the term influence in her PhD dissertation based on a critical reading of the contributions of Harold Bloom as "stimulating burden," "creative interpretation," "poetic appropriation" and mainly, as choice – of the part of the influenced – and not as imposition or transposition (term that suggests a certain passive inevitability on the part of those who *suffer* the process). Influence does not need to result in the reduction of value of the creative act, and it is the more present the stronger the poet – and/or the architect is. See: Zein, "A arquitetura da escola paulista brutalista 1953-1973" (PhD diss., UFRGS, 2005, www.lume.ufrgs.br/handle/10183/5452); Harold Bloom, *A angústia da influência. Uma teoria da poesia* (Rio de Janeiro: Imago, 2002), 23-24.

5. T.N.: From the phrase apocryphally said by Galileu Galilei, after apostatizing his heliocentric hypothesis *eppur si muove* (and yet it is in movement).

6. Evidently, theories do not think; in order to be subtle, the text operates a prosopopoeia. Human beings, and that includes academic researchers, are often reluctant to revise their own set of truths. Unfortunately, the more experienced an author is, the more the situation worsens: If one has already published a lot, any change would turn his/her previous texts anachronistic. If so, new innovative research tends at best to be disturbing, at worst to be infuriating. Although accepting that that's how human nature works, one is obliged to remember the subversive nature of true research. And better be prepared because sooner or later, our own pet theories will eventually be overturned.

7. Another common recurrent question come from those who state that it is not wise to say these (subversive) stuff because it may be misinterpreted by students and others. This is a critique of moral judgment that cannot be considered under penalty of eliminating research, and even writing, since everything can be misinterpreted in life.

8. As defined in earlier texts by the author: Zein, "A arquitetura da escola paulista brutalista 1953-1973"; Zein, "Brutalismo, sobre sua definição (ou, de como um rótulo superficial é, por isso mesmo, adequado)," *Arquitextos* 084.00, May 2007, www.vitruvius.com.br/revistas/read/arquitextos/07.084/243.

9. A partial version of this text was presented at the *Cardinal Points of Architectural Theory 1920-1950 International Seminar* and was published in its annals (Universidad Nacional de Rosário, 2011). The presentation was followed by a rich, intense critical discussion that doubtlessly contributed to the revision and precision of the present text. Even if the same phenomenon of an a priori rejection of my proposals had taken place then, the direct clash with intellectual colleagues who disagreed with my positions was extremely useful to me. Anyway, that confirmed that an a priori non acceptance, based on deeply rooted ideological convictions, that they who criticize didn't want to question for political or ordinary reasons, were not just a figment of my imagination.

IT AIN'T NECESSARILY SO...

(HAVE YOU EVER HEARD OF VILANOVA ARTIGAS?)

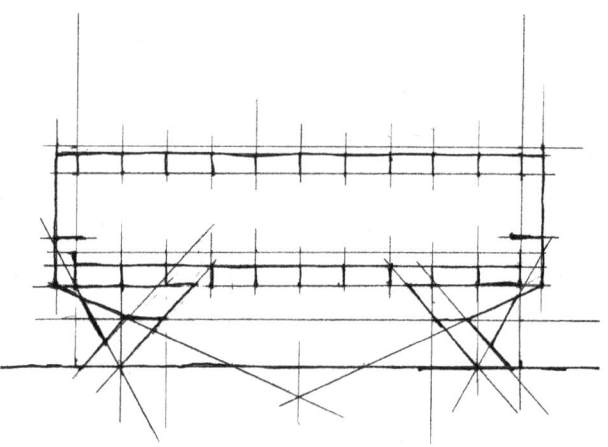

São Paulo Soccer Club's locker room, construction scheme of the transverse section, São Paulo SP. Vilanova Artigas, 1960.
Drawing Ruth Verde Zein

Brazil is a huge country and its multifaceted modern architecture comprises a large variety of remarkable personages and buildings that are worth (re)considering in the composition of a truly worldwide account of the best 20th century modern architecture. Until recently, only Brazil's classical *carioca*[1] modernism of the 1930-50s had been more widely acknowledged abroad, followed by an inexplicable void. After the 1990s, the worldwide reconnaissance of the outstanding work of architect Lina Bo Bardi has helped to gradually overcome that gap. Nowadays, at least two other remarkable Brazilians/*paulistas* modern generation architects are also getting recognition for their work: The 2006 Pritker Prize Paulo Mendes da Rocha; and recently, for the enjoyment of a more selected group of connoisseurs, the late architect João Batista Vilanova Artigas.

Vilanova Artigas (1915-85) was a most prolific modern architect. He began his professional activities in 1938 and assumed a prominent architectural role in the 1960s. He graduated as an engineer-architect at the Polytechnic School of São Paulo in 1937. Partner of Marone & Artigas project & construction office (1938-44) and owner of Vilanova Artigas Architecture after 1944. Professor at the University of São Paulo since 1944. Affiliated to the Brazilian Communist Party since 1945. Travelled thorough US thanks to a Guggenheim Foundation Grant (1947-48). After 1960 he assumed a prominent role in the renovation of the architectural courses, before being expelled from the university for political reasons (1969-80) and resumed his position after the political amnesty. Initially influenced by Frank Lloyd Wright, and then by the modern *carioca* school, in the end of the 1950s his mature work assumed a brutalist streak and became very influential in São Paulo and beyond. Also an artist and a writer, his political militant texts counterpoint with his erudite lessons on architecture and design. Despite having produced hundreds of buildings of excellent technical and formal inventiveness, the recognition of his work is yet limited in Brazil and abroad to a handful of canonical buildings. His varied and complex professional life, spanning from the 1940s to the 1980s, is often narrowly identified with a supposed *paulista* school, a somewhat reductive historical construct of fuzzy temporal and conceptual borders.

Since the quality of his works and his notorious professional, professorial and political militancy is being well acknowledged in Brazil and abroad, Artigas may not be considered a completely unknown personage, whose reputation should be established or revealed. On the other hand, his career, works and deeds have been strained by critics, writers and historians as to fit him into several entangled layers of given interpretations that have paradoxically accumulated over the personages, somehow impairing the reconnaissance of his architectural contribution in itself, or at least, outside these stratified clichés.

In order to properly ensure the understanding of the importance and quality of his work without lightly or hastily endorsing the current ideological fixed interpretations of his life and time, it is necessary to revise how Artigas has been understood, interpreted and treated by successive critics and historians that helped to construct his contemporary *persona*. In order to try and accomplish that, one has to briefly step back to the 1940s and recap how the construction of the *genius* paradigm, to explain the burst of modern architecture in Brazil, was counterpointed by the emergence of supposed antagonists and how, despite himself, Artigas became one of them.

Then, it would be necessary to understand how the dissolution of the *carioca* Brazilian unity/identity paradigm in the 1960s was partially denied or compensated by the admission of a roughly complementary and mirroring *paulista* school. After that, how the historiographical construct of a brutalist *paulista* school in the 1955-75 period, had its historical boundaries artificially expanded, spilling over the 1980s-90s decades, and landing in the contemporary realm, in order to become a kind of generic, jack-of-all-trades label, the *paulista* school: A most imprecise historiographical category with no clear temporal or formal frontiers, that despite its scant consistency has acquired a high national – and recently, international – credibility.

Finally, how the advent of a new generation of young talented Brazilian architects and their organic critics are reclaiming a personal and distilled version of Artigas heritage, sanctioning their own prestige by revivifying some of the 1960s *ethical* debates, perhaps to give a spice to the conservative, reductive, imaginative imagistic and shallow contemporary architectural debates.

It's probably very complicated to try to properly compress all this information, in a brief paper. But let's do it, beginning in the 1940s.

GENIUSES ARE MADE IN HEAVEN

In 1947, the architecture magazine *Anteprojeto*, edited by the students of the School of Architecture at the National University in Rio de Janeiro, published a report on "Brazilian Contemporary Architecture" dedicated to "architect Lúcio Costa, master of traditional architecture and pioneer of contemporary architecture in Brazil."[2] This unassuming homage triggered a controversy that led to the establishment of a very persistent historiographical paradigm, that rested undisputed for decades and is still evoked today.

The controversy was flared when São Paulo's critic and journalist Geraldo Ferraz disputed the pioneering status of Costa as a gross "sleight of the historical truth [ignoring] the primacy manifested in São Paulo by Gregori Warchavchik and Flavio de Carvalho." In his opinion, that repeated the mistake of MoMA NY exhibition

Brazil Builds catalogue; so he dared Lúcio Costa to step forward and "re-establish the hierarchy of events in the exact order in which they had happened."[3]

In his reply Costa did not endorse Ferraz complaints. He accepted that his friend and ex-partner Warchavchik had actually designed after 1927 the first modernist houses in Brazil and he recognized the "shattering action" of Carvalho's art/architecture happenings. But for Costa, those were not the most important mile-

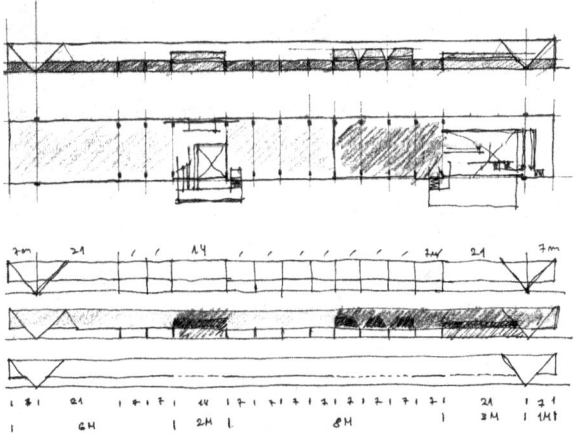

São Paulo Soccer Club's locker room, front elevation, first floor plan and construction scheme of the front elevation, São Paulo SP. Vilanova Artigas, 1960. Drawing Ruth Verde Zein

stones to understand contemporary (1948) Brazilian modern architecture, as they were not instrumental in the launching of its huge international appraisal in the immediate postwar period. For Costa, such appraisal happened due to a completely different, exceptional and unique reason: The sheer manifestation of the geniality of a most gifted architect, namely, Oscar Niemeyer.[4]

Shifting the focus from himself to his *protégé*, Costa disregarded the importance of the timeline pace of events in the construction of a narrative able to encompass Brazilian modern architecture. Instead, he poured the whole weight of history on the sudden burst of a genius, an event that defied any rational explanation and was not prone to be easily repeated. Brazil's inclusion in the ranks of modern architecture as a fortuitous exception was a strategic move: A polite diplomatic solution to settle the uncomfortable question proposed by the existence of a Brazilian modernity, without questioning the validity of the avant-garde discourse about modernity as a byproduct of advanced industrialization.

THAT CONCILIATORY IDEA HAS PROSPERED:
FROM THEN ON, INSIDE AND OUTSIDE THE
COUNTRY, BRAZILIAN MODERN ARCHITECTURE
WOULD ONCE AND AGAIN BE IDENTIFIED

and almost exclusively reduced by commentators, critics and historians to the works and deeds of just one genius architect. As so, in Brazil and abroad, some direct or indirect reference to Niemeyer became obligatory even when the subject was the work of any other local professional. In addition, when local/foreign critics wished to be polemical, they had only to favor another Brazilian architect, emphasizing his/her real or supposed differences with Niemeyer's attitude and works. And Affonso Eduardo Reidy was probably one of the preferred nemesis in those reductive and bipolar faux disputes.

Costa's intention was not to minimize other architects' contributions. His quest had a more strategic and political nature, and included the consolidation of an idea of a *modern national architecture identity*.

Oscar Niemeyer original transmutation of Le Corbusier's plastic vocabulary may have seemed to Lúcio Costa as the answer to a local expression, a fruitful synthesis between national and international, tradition and modernity, an enriching contribution to the vocabulary of the discipline.[5]

Comas adds other layers of subtlety to this interpretation:

[Brazilian modern architecture] success abroad grants its emblem potential, and contributes to its hegemony from 1950 on. The Brazilian modern architecture will become an ensign of a nationalism that flares up in a cold war climate, as the regressive idea of a backward country is replaced by the idea of an underdeveloped Third World country. To the right-wing politics, nationalism is interesting because it enables the cultural homogenization demanded by the industrialization process, in terms of labor force or consumer market. To the left-wing, nationalism is interesting as reaction to the passive integration into the Western bloc.[6]

After that, any attempt to enlarge the field by adding other architects' names and works to the history of Brazilian architecture was frequently (mis)read as a dispute over Niemeyer's preeminence. The obvious and superior qualities of Niemeyer's works helped consolidate the myth, for his projects were unquestionably daring, interesting and innovative enough to make us all Brazilians proud of him. On the other hand, any effort to broaden the panorama into a more inclusive ensemble was also prone to be (mis)read as an attempt of fracturing the *unity* of Brazilian modern architecture *identity*. Something that neither the rightist architects, historians, and critics nor the leftist ones would want to happen, as Comas explained above.

UNDERCURRENTS BELLOW A BED OF ROSES

Although the Brazilian modern architecture identity/unity paradigm gained status as an almost official interpretation, counterpoints, sometimes more other times less explicit, kept coming almost immediately, from outside and inside the country. A most interesting case is the contribution of Lina Bo Bardi in presenting João Baptista Vilanova Artigas as a sort of Brazilian/*paulista* antithesis of the Brazilian/*carioca* modern architecture.

A few years after migrating to Brazil, Pietro Maria and Lina Bo Bardi launched *Habitat*, a "magazine for arts and architecture"[7] which published the first efforts of an *independent* criticism on Brazilian architecture, meant here as adopting an attitude that was not political or doctrinally engaged with the construction of a *national* narrative, neither affiliated to a marxist discourse, nor stuck in a trade union defense of the architect profession. Acting as a kind of cultural snipers with moving targets, both Bardi along with their local and international friends published articles in *Habitat* enthusiastically praising Brazilian *carioca* architecture school while subtly poking its supposed weaknesses. And perhaps to show their discomfort with Rio de Janeiro's predominance in Brazilian modern architecture, they chose to display some houses designed by João Batista Vilanova

Artigas on the cover and in the main article of *Habitat*'s first issue (1950).

Born in Curitiba in 1915 from a workers' family, Artigas came to São Paulo in the 1930s to study architecture at the Polytechnic School of Engineering, becoming an engineer-architect in 1938. After a decade of professional experience designing and constructing relatively small buildings for private clients, from the mid-1940s on Artigas works became sort of realigned and phased with the Brazilian modern architecture of the *carioca* school, without completely losing his initial wrightian elective affiliation, a trait Artigas kept alive until his last works. At that moment of the publication in *Habitat* he also frequented local artistic circles, being an excellent draftsman himself, engaged in professional debates and call for actions as the creation of the local Brazilian Institute of Architects – IAB, and began a long-term relationship with the (then proscribed) Communist Party. For a brief period, he worked with Gregori Warchavchik in a prestigious competition for a (never built) São Paulo City Hall. When his houses were published in 1950s *Habitat*, he had already won a Guggenheim Grant which allowed him and his wife Virginia, also an artist, to travel coast to coast in the United States for a year (1947-48). In addition to this, by 1950 some of his works had already been published abroad, a feat until then shared only by a few senior and very prestigious local colleagues like Rino Levi, Gregori Warchavchik, and Oswaldo Bratke.

Despite that impressive résumé for such a (then) young talented architect, with no strong family ties to enable his professional career, Lina Bo Bardi began her article "Casas de Artigas"[8] (Artigas' houses) in *Habitat* 1 with a kind of psychological description of the architect, and I quote: "Artigas is a withdrawn person who likes to live in the shadows, who does not appear in magazines, and does not like to publish." Such almost fictional argument was fabricated by Lina in order to affirm that Artigas "dislikes publishing projects, ideas, drawings [because] for him architecture is a built work, a finished result, after every detail had already been settled." In the third sentence Lina reached the main stream of her critical analysis, by relating Vilanova Artigas works with the values of "humanity and domesticity." Such characteristics would be manifested by some absent qualities, for Artigas' houses, according to her, "do not follow the laws dictated by life routines [...] they are not flashy, nor they impose a semblance of modernity, something that today may already be defined as a styling [...] they do not deplete themselves in a single pleasurable sensation of an exterior architecture." Artigas architecture would be "almost always severe, puritanical" and also "moral." To inaugurate her new magazine, she did not choose to publish some "fanciful, novel, modern and different architecture [...] transformed into fashion design" – epithets used in a veiled mention to the *carioca* modernity. Instead, *Habitat* chose to favor some good pieces of modern architecture that were not the result of merely formal exercises.

Interestingly enough and despite the natural differences of place and climate, a close reading of Artigas houses of that period would show more proximities than distances from the design procedures of the *carioca* school, as the changes in his work, swerving away from the *carioca* modernism into a *brutalist* attitude, will happen only a decade later. On the other hand, Artigas was then, in 1950, already a very active public person, notwithstanding his (then hidden) connections with the proscribed Communist Party – although he would only later, in the 1960s, assume a marked preeminence in the local production. So, from any objective point of view, Lina's interpretation in *Habitat* 1 is more fictional than factual; but anyway, the die was cast. The tag of a shadowy and withdrawn person designing *moral* houses and buildings would happily haunt his career until after his demise in the 1980s, and even today.

Regardless of the intrinsic qualities of his works, Artigas was not the only *enfant terrible* or *bogey* target fabricated by Brazilian and international critics to unsettle the preeminence of Niemeyer and the *carioca* modern school. To make a long and complex story short, at least until the inauguration of Brasília (1960), a simplified interpretative panorama was already made available for the use of the regular (and superficial) understanding of Brazilian modern architecture. Above, there was the explicit and praised preeminence of Oscar Niemeyer as a native genius, growing steadier with Papadaki's book[9] and fluctuating with the construction of the new Brazilian capital. By counterpoint, any other Brazilian architect, no matter where she/he practiced, was tainted by a sort of invisibility cloak that made him/her position to be always interpreted as either a secondary follower or an outsider contestant. Some very talented architects like the *carioca* Affonso Eduardo Reidy and the *paulista* Vilanova Artigas, who would have their prestige recognized in itself in many other circumstances, were instead considered as a sort of Niemeyer's nemesis, in reductive and bipolar faux disputes. In any case, what was (or still is) constantly absent in the scene was a dispassionate and careful analysis of the works themselves, as produced by all these personages – including Niemeyer's – either before or after the assumption of any a priori ready-made interpretation. And that is not a secondary effect:

THE HISTORIOGRAPHY OF BRAZILIAN MODERN ARCHITECTURE AND ITS POSITION IN THE 20TH CENTURY GLOBAL PANORAMA HAS BEEN PERMANENTLY STRICKEN, AT LEAST UNTIL VERY RECENTLY, BY SUCH STAGNANT ASSUMPTIONS AND PERPLEXING ABSENCES.

Vilanova Artigas reputational fortune gradually *changed* in the mature moments of his professional career. In the 1960s he gained a local, and after the 1980s, a national preeminence, mostly due to the daring and boldness quality of his brutalist architectural production. At that moment his prestige tide turned and another historiographical construction is put forward: That of Vilanova Artigas as the presumed leader of the *paulista* brutalist school, which, once again, is not a completely accurate interpretation. That aspect needs some effort to be disentangled which can only be done here in a very brief way.

THE INVENTION OF THE 'PAULISTA'/BRUTALIST SCHOOL

In her article "A idéia de uma identidade *paulista* na historiografia de arquitetura brasileira,"[10] Dedecca states that "São Paulo architects/ architecture emerge as a theme in the architecture historiography [only] in the mid-1960s, as part of a broader debate about the Brazilian modern architecture, when the primacy of the *carioca* school is fading."[11] Actually, a most singular time overlapping happens in the 1960s, although probably with no single cause/effect connections among all events: The fading of the *carioca* school, the inauguration of Brasília, the insurgence of *paulista* brutalist trend in the late 1950s, and some years late the wretched military coup in Brazil (1964).

A new generation of talented architects graduating after 1955 would open the so-called brutalist scene in São Paulo with some exemplary works.[12] Initiated by the younger architects the trend was then closely followed by the shift of an older generation of architects to reinforce the brutalist ranks by their timely realignment. And Vilanova Artigas was certainly one of its most important (but not the only) personage. After an initial (until ~1944) wrightian and second (until 1956) corbusian-*carioca* phases, Vilanova Artigas begins to produce some of the most remarkable exposed concrete buildings of daring structural and formal character, especially after 1959. Due to his seniority, larger experience, professorial and professional consolidated status, he was then in a proper position to assume, in the next decade, a most important and exemplary role in the 1960s *paulista* architectural practice.

Despite the regular publication of his works in local journals and some brief mentions of Artigas brutalism in international magazines,[13] a more concerted account on the work of his brutalist phase and the reconnaissance of his gradually more preeminent position in the 1960s was initially proposed by the French historian Yves Bruand in his doctoral dissertation *Contemporary Architecture in Brazil*.[14] Bruand's account on 20th century Brazilian architecture mostly followed the already existing established interpretations of its *carioca identity*, confirming the *genius* paradigm, but the French historian also tried to enlarge the panorama by encompassing other personages and works. In the last part of his thesis, Bruand acknowledged the differences between the 1940s-50s and the 1960s Brazilian architecture, and the geographical shifting of interest from Rio de Janeiro to São Paulo. But since the predominant historiographical paradigm that he (implicitly) adopted was grounded on the defense of the *unity/identity* of Brazilian modern architecture, he chose to explain the differences while "solidify[ing] the clash between Rio's and Artigas's production, even suggesting a *rivalry*, thus consolidating one of the most influential readings, [from then on], constantly revisited, about that [São Paulo] ambitious production."[15]

Bruand's European cultural background possibly granted him an atavistic respect for the elders, so he could not avoid but to interpret Artigas position in the 1960s as that of a veritable *chef de file* of a *paulista* brutalist school, suggesting the existence of a professor/disciple relationship between Artigas and several other talented younger architects of the local generation. That was not quite a precise interpretation: The majority of the 1950s-60s talented young architects quoted by Bruand had not been Vilanova Artigas' students, and had begun their professional careers simultaneously or even before Artigas shift into a more stark brutalist language.[16]

IT AIN'T NECESSARILY SO...

HOWEVER, AND THIS TIME AGAIN, THE ACTUAL PACE OF THE EVENTS WAS DISREGARDED AND GRANTED LESS IMPORTANCE THAN THE SPROUTING OF A LOCAL PRODIGY, SOMEHOW MIRRORING THE TYPIFIED THEORETICAL STRUCTURE OF THE 'CARIOCA' SCHOOL.

However in this case the symmetry was not so perfect: *Genius* was replaced by the *mentor*, and the role of Lúcio Costa as the intellectual leader and Oscar Niemeyer as the talented designer were both to be attributed, in São Paulo, to Vilanova Artigas.

Anyway, by no means these necessary precisions on the historiographical invention of the *paulista* school are meant to diminish the importance of Vilanova Artigas contribution to Brazilian architecture in the 1960s. On the contrary: A more ample and concerted research on the repertoire of the *paulista* brutalist trend shows that in the 1960s he was single-handedly responsible for designing the majority of that period's noteworthy buildings.[17] Besides, a slightly later generation of *paulista* architects entering the scene after ~1965 would assume Artigas as their role-model master, and part of an even later generation of the 1980s-90s would choose consider themselves as his *posthumous disciples* – since some of them had had a most brief contact with him and many others, null personal contact.

WHEN ARTIGAS RISES, BRAZIL VANISHES FROM THE SCENE

Despite the flaws of Bruand's historiographical narratives, a systematic study and close reading of the wide examples repertoire of the 1960s erudite Brazilian modern architecture would confirm that Vilanova Artigas had had then an undeniable protagonist role. Nevertheless, such finding was not clearly acknowledged in Brazil until the 1980s, and abroad only after the 2000s.

But in the second half of the 20th century, contrary to what had happened in the 1940s-50s, a complex set of circumstances – like a general prejudice against Brasília and the rising criticism against modern architecture's shortcomings – contributed to the lessening of the interest on Brazilian architecture by international critics, historians and editors after the 1960s-70s. The breach of the sympathy towards Brazil worsened after 1964s *coup d'état*, when the country became ruled by a right-wing military dictatorship. The new authoritarian and technocratic regime did not actually impair the work of most architects: Instead, it promoted a slew of public works throughout the country, engaging the majority of Brazilian architects, of all political colors. But the human rights abuses were intolerable to most critics and editors of that time's major international magazines, deriving in a pervading rejection against Brazilian architecture, whose feats practically disappeared from the international radar screen.

Despite Artigas leftist political position, reinforced by the UIA's Jean Tschumi Prize for Architectural Education he received in 1972 – that somehow certified his non-compliance with the Brazilian right-wing dictatorship – his works, and those of several other *paulista* architects, designed during or immediately after the construction of Brasília, remained internationally unaccounted and unrecognized, until recently. During almost the entire second half of the 20th century, Brazilian modern architecture was referred to in line with a much worn and almost mythical account of the classical/*carioca* modern that was briefly included in the canonical histories of architecture manuals, treated as a transitory and almost mythical episode; while for decades, post-Brasília modern Brazilian architecture remained ignored.[18]

Before and after his appearance in *Habitat* 1, Vilanova Artigas works were regularly, even if sparingly, published in local and international journals. But his reputation only began to grow, after he had designed the new building of the School of Architecture and Urbanism of the São Paulo University – FAU USP (1961-69), despite (and because of) his political-driven removal (1969) from his position there as a professor. In 1980 the political amnesty brought Artigas back to the university. In 1981, Bruand's research was published in Portuguese;[19] a book reuniting some of Artigas political and aesthetical texts was also published in the same year.[20] The first monographic books focusing on the study of his work from a formal, constructive and architectural point of view gained national notoriety only after 1984.[21]

The political amnesty and the publication of his recollected texts brought his until then semi-occult militant and partisan life to the center of the arena. Such disclosure stimulated the imagination of some critics, prompting them to suggest that the basis of Vilanova Artigas architectural creativity derived from his political positions, and should be sought outside the disciplinary field of architecture. Despite its conceptual feebleness, such political interpretative bias gradually gained preeminence, with some critics going so far as to consider Artigas works *partis* and detailing as a byproduct of his political beliefs. Quoting again Dedecca, as if "his [Artigas] political action, in face of architecture, [would] emerge as the axis for understanding his [design] trajectory."[22]

Artigas himself partially fueled this strain of interpretation in some spoken interviews he had given just before his demise (1985). His last words proposed a retrospective and somewhat disenchanted view of his own trajectory, and are not at all necessarily congruent with his previous attitudes and beliefs, as they had happened along the five decades of his professional career. Alas, consolidating this warped interpretation, the first panoramic book on his work published in 1997 smartly edited and scattered those last words along the book, juxtaposing his last words with images of his 1940s-70s buildings, changing their weight and significance, creating fictional anachronistic links that favored the political/ architectural conjunction interpretation. Afterwards, the book's anachronistic accounts were translated into other languages and quoted in local and international studies.[23] Such trustful but non-critical repetition reinforced the legend making it almost *official*. From a rigorous historiographical point of view such manipulation of the facts resulted in an authentic trap: A false truth, but very complicated to disentangle and almost impossible to question without – somehow – tainting the master's image.

AS THE 'PAULISTA' SCHOOL GETS INTERNATIONAL IT BECOMES A TRINITY

The resurgence and appraisal of Brazilian late modern architecture in the international scenario was resumed after the 1990s. It had opportunely begun with the reconnaissance of the outstanding work of Lina Bo Bardi as architect and designer; after her, decades of silence and disinterest gradually fell apart. In this wake, at least two other very important modern-generation Brazilian/

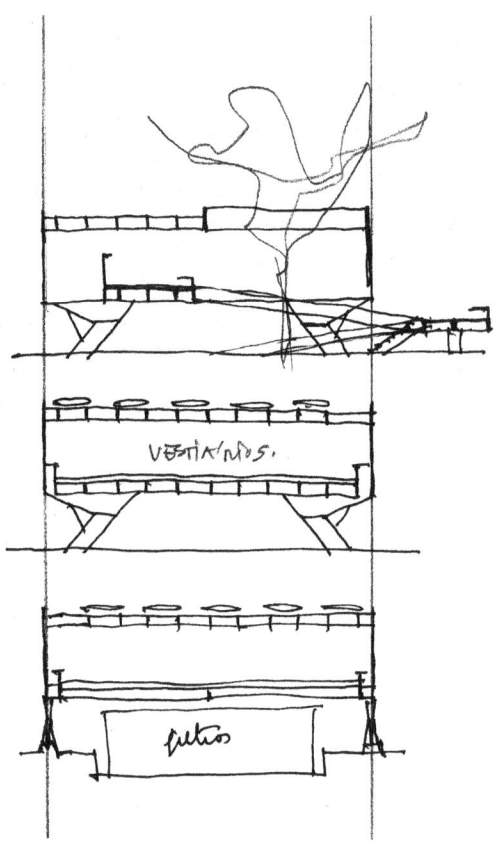

São Paulo Soccer Club's locker room, transverse sections, São Paulo SP. Vilanova Artigas, 1960. Drawing Ruth Verde Zein *paulista* architects had their works widely recognized and praised: First Paulo Mendes da Rocha, still alive, actively producing, and 2006 Pritker Prize winner; and lately, for the enjoyment of a more selected group of connoisseurs, João Batista Vilanova Artigas.

Lina's role of *agent provocateur* in the 1950s, her circumstance as émigré, her feminine condition (against the prejudices of that moment still provincial-minded city of São Paulo) and the radicalism of her positions did not help her to establish a regular professional practice as a designer until very late in her life. But although she had produced some remarkable projects and buildings, her works were conspicuously ignored by her local fellow architects until the 1980s. Levered by the inauguration of the SESC Pompeia Leisure Centre (1985), a new generation of critics and historians helped to transmute such unfair oblivion into a deserved recognition. A wave of scholar and editorial appreciation revised her earlier and later projects, helping invert the prestige tide; and the daring boldness of her works finally earned worldwide recognition. For the sake of brevity, it would not be possible to further linger into the very interesting case of Mendes da Rocha, whose deserved growing prestige after the 21st century may signalize a change in the mood in both the Pritzker Prize and the world architecture ambiance as well.

After Artigas' works and professional trajectory gained international disclosure, the tale of the duality between a *paulista* school and a *carioca* school also gained notoriety, and implicitly, fostered the image of Vilanova Artigas as an iconic leader, and as a sort of complementary iconic image to counterweight the Niemeyer/Costa set. Likewise, Artigas new prestige tide was partially built over the flimsy but paradoxically convincing idea of an epic personage that was able to give credibility to an allegedly close connection between his political action and his architectural design process. Certainly, many of the best Brazilian and international commentators have not easily slipped into such *naïve faux pas*. But if the stuff of legends is made in the silence of cabinets, its spreading is confirmed by the murmur of the crowd. A price was paid. The disruption of the shadows that had once covered Brazilian modern/late modern architecture, whose previous reconnaissance had been laced by the mark of exception, geniality and fanciness, did not exactly help uncover all those myths. Instead, new layers of novel myths did come up.

But despite the inevitable flaws that the feebleness of human nature will always spread over any historiographical narratives, the works and buildings of João Batista Vilanova Artigas, Brazilian and *paulista* architect, deserve to be recognized, studied, praised and included in the Olympus of the best modern architects of the 20th century. Preferably, without adjective appendices such as *regionalist* or *ethnic*. These labels seem to signal a possible inclusion when they are, in fact, a veiled and *politically correct* exclusion. As his fellow modern architects of the mid-20th century from everywhere, Vilanova Artigas in his works seemed to have aspired to balance universal and local, in search of a utopic, unattainable equilibrium; and to do so in a most bold and affirmative way.

Perhaps the best scenario to avoid the mystification of star-architects is to insist on the study and unbiased appreciation of their buildings. The rising or declining of an architect's reputation, inside or outside his country or region, may not necessarily be the best grounds for a deep understanding of his/her still unappreciated architectural landmarks. As it happens, both things cannot be easily untangled; so a double effort should conduct the uncovering of new prestige subjects.

The legend of *moral* Artigas, put forward by Lina, ratified by Bruand and enhanced by several other contemporary authors has always worked as an apt tactic to frame Vilanova Artigas' contemporary reputation under an almost folkloric leftist discourse identity. A reputation that, in a certain way, overshadows and reduces the complexities and contradictions of his professional life and works. And perhaps, Vilanova Artigas buildings are far more interesting to get to know than the one-dimensional personage of the legends.

NOTES

EN. Article originally presented at the Society of Architectural Historians – SAH Conference (Pasadena, April 2016).

1. TN: *Carioca* refers to what or who is natural of Rio de Janeiro.

2. Alberto Xavier, ed., *Lúcio Costa: sobre arquitetura* (Porto Alegre: Centro dos Estudantes Universitários de Arquitetura, 1962), 119.

3. Ibid., 122. Originally published in: Geraldo Ferraz, "Falta o depoimento de Lúcio Costa," *Diário de São Paulo*, February 1st, 1948.

4. Ibid., 198. Free translation. Costa will reinforce his argument in the text "Depoimento de um arquiteto carioca," of 1951. Ibid., 169-201.

5. Maria Alice Junqueira Bastos and Ruth Verde Zein, *Brasil: arquiteturas após 1950* (São Paulo: Perspectiva, 2010), 31.

6. Carlos Eduardo Dias Comas, "Brazil Builds e a bossa barroca: notas sobre a singularização da arquitetura moderna brasileira," *6° Seminário DOCOMOMO Brasil* (Niterói: DOCOMOMO, 2005).

7. Ruth Verde Zein, "Habitat, Lina Bo Bardi y la Crítica de Arquitectura no Alineada," *Summa+* 101, 2009, 32-41.

8. Lina Bo Bardi, "Casas de Artigas," *Habitat* 1, 2.

9. Stamo Papadaki, *The Work of Oscar Niemeyer* (New York: Reinhold, 1950).

10. Paula Gorenstein Dedecca, "A idéia de uma identidade paulista na historiografia de arquitetura brasileira," *Revista Pós* 19/32, December 2012.

11. Ibid., 94.

12. Actually, some of the first brutalist buildings in Brazil were designed by the *carioca* Affonso Eduardo Reidy, like the MAM of Rio de Janeiro (1953).

13. Bruno Alfieri, "Ricerca Brutalista," *Zodiac* 6, 1960, 97.

14. Yves Bruand, *Arquitetura contemporânea no Brasil* (São Paulo: Perspectiva, 2010).

15. Ibid., 96.

16. Ruth Verde Zein, "A arquitetura da escola paulista brutalista 1953-1973" (PhD diss., UFRGS, 2005), http://www.lume.ufrgs.br/handle/10183/5452.

17. Ibid.

18. Ruth Verde Zein, "Brazil Architecture 1955-1980," in: *Latin American in Construction: Architecture 1955-1980*, eds. Barry Bergdoll, Carlos Eduardo Dias Comas, Jorge Francisco Liernur and Patricio del Real (New York: MoMA, 2015).

19. The original text in French was available at the FAU USP library just after its completion in 1974.

20. João Batista Vilanova Artigas, *Caminhos da arquitetura* (São Paulo: Lech, 1981).

21. Ruth Verde Zein, "Vilanova Artigas; a obra do arquiteto," *Projeto* 66, August 1984, 79-91.

22. Dedecca, "A idéia de uma identidade paulista," 97.

23. Hugo Segawa, "Vilanova Artigas, o renascer de um mestre," *Resenhas Online* 001.21, Vitruvius, January 2002, http://www.vitruvius.com.br/revistas/read/resenhasonline/01.001/3258.

BREUER AFFECTIONS, BACK AND FORTH

SOME CHOSEN SCENARIOS

MARCEL BREUER APPEARS VERY EARLY IN 20TH CENTURY MODERN ARCHITECTURE AVANT-GARDE SCENARIO AND HIS NOTEWORTHY WORK AS DESIGNER, ARCHITECT, WRITER AND CONSTRUCTOR PERSIST THOROUGH HIS PROFESSIONAL CAREER. HIS DISCREET PRESENCE IS NEVERTHELESS INDISPENSABLE: HE SEEMS TO BE ALWAYS AT THE RIGHT PLACE, ON THE RIGHT TIME, DOING THE RIGHT THING, praised as an uncontroversial figure with a crucial, albeit coadjuvant role. At least, from 1920 to 1976, the years of his admission as a student in Bauhaus and of his retirement, as senior partner of a successful design company based in the USA with a significant international portfolio. In between, Breuer's creativity underwent distinct phases displaying different artistic and architectural proposals, in an ample variety of forms and scopes; so that he truly impersonates the myth of the modern architect, able to design "from the spoon to the city;" or in his case, from chairs to major government buildings.

However, a careful reviewing of the main 20th-century architecture history manuals in search of architect Marcel Breuer's works and deeds would find only a few scattered and recurrent references. His works after the UNESCO Building (Paris, 1954), with the exception of the Whitney Museum (New York, 1963-66), are seldom mentioned in the canonical architectural history books written after the 1980s. Oddly enough, at the 1960s-70s Breuer was at the peak of his professional career, having his works regularly published in most international journals and having the comprehensive books on his works and ideas widely studied, admired and emulated, all over the world.

There is no doubt on the relevance of his contributions, but the recognition of his merits still remains stuck before his

1960s works, and mostly on the early and very bright beginning of his career, when his artistic creativity was focused on furniture and interior design. Already in the 1920s-30s he created objects that turned into undisputed classics and performed as exemplarily demonstrations of the possibilities of industrial design and serial production. His creations helped to consolidate the Bauhaus innovative image, as much as the buildings proposed by Walter Gropius and the other professors. Quickly and brilliantly moving forward from student to teacher, Marcel Breuer's Bauhaus creations were probably able to inspire his own masters – one could not imagine Mies van der Rohe's Barcelona's or Charlotte Perriand/Le Corbusier chairs without Breuer's prior contribution.

Like other architects of his generation he only manages to build his ideas in the next decade, just before leaving nazi Germany on account of his Jewish origin.[1] A brief stay in London in 1935-37 earned him some architectural works. It was the precise moment that local historians tend to consider as the fertile beginning of England's modern architecture, with the temporary presence of other foreign architects like Berthold Lubetkin, Eric Mendelsohn, Serge Chermayeff and even Walter Gropius himself. The next step for both Breuer and Gropius, and soon to be followed by other personalities of the former Bauhaus, was their relocation in the United States. In 1937 Gropius took over as dean of the architecture department of the Harvard University in Cambridge, asks Breuer to join the school team and invites him to share a professional partnership.

Gropius contribution to architectural education it is widely considered and highly appreciated, from Bauhaus to America. Alas, the same protagonist role cannot be attributed to his American architectural works, which had never obtained the prestige attached to his name as an educator. Anyway, their professional association will not last: Breuer quits the partnership in 1941. Accepted as a minor associate by the elder and grander colleague, Breuer was nevertheless the most creative half of the pair – as can be inferred from the results of their subsequent architectural careers after their parting. Older than Breuer, Gropius was perhaps less able to adapt his design traits to the new requirements and possibilities available in the United States. Hitchcock believes that "the houses that Breuer designed after separating from Gropius have considerable greater intrinsic interest; and as it would perhaps be more natural in the case of a younger man, his [houses] soon showed a more integral adjustment to the characteristic lifestyle and construction methods of the New World."[2]

After 1946 Breuer leaves Harvard and establishes his office in New York; it's when he then designs and builds his American

Houses, putting himself in the front lines of the *avant-garde* debates on housing, in the USA East Coast – an individualistic and middle-class approach when compared to Europe's post-war counterpart, characterized by massive housing proposals and debates. And perhaps because he was not one of *the big* masters (sparing the museum the trouble of handling mutual jealousies), and was there right at hand, it's Breuer's house prototype that was chosen by the MoMA – The Museum of Modern Art, in New York – to be exposed in its sculpture garden in 1949, with the title *Model House to the Modern American Family*.[3] It was visited by "about 75 thousand people, a record for the season"[4] and inaugurated just after the exhibition *From Le Corbusier to Niemeyer: 1929-1949*.[5] Afterwards that prestigious museum – a well-known launcher of architectural fashions – organized a traveling exhibition on Breuer's works, further promoting their visibility and exemplary role.

The years just before and after the MoMa exhibition until the invitation to design the UNESCO building in Paris (1953-58, with Bernard Zehrfuss and Pier Luigi Nervi) Breuer was considered as a "house-architect" – as he complains in his book,[6] published in a moment that he is trying to go beyond that label and to launch his international career. Still today, for the majority of the critics and historians, Breuer's American houses of the 1944-60 period were the best examples of his architectural creativity. Quoting again Hitchcock, "if there was a *school* [in post-Second World War USA] it would be that of Gropius [...] but the work itself of the *gropiusians*, so to call them, in fact derives much more from the practice of his former disciple and partner Breuer, than from himself."[7]

THE AVAILABLE REFERENCES ABOUT MARCEL BREUER IN MOST CANONICAL HISTORY BOOKS STOP THERE, IN THE LATE 1950S. ODDLY ENOUGH, IT WAS AFTER THAT MOMENT THAT HALF OF HIS PROJECTS WERE MEANT TO BE DESIGNED:

> His third and brutalist last phase is, quantitatively speaking, his more productive one. But the last twenty years Marcel Breuer works (1956-76) are not quite properly unknown, since they were *pari passu* widely published in almost all architectural journals of the world and in his own books. And his brutalist constructive, compositional and aesthetic propositions also did school, and were appropriated by several epigones all over the world, and even by some brilliant (and yet not acknowledged) *indirect* disciples. Still, recent studies on his work do not fully acknowledge the importance and quality of his last phase, which still remains to be systematically revised from a contemporary critical stand.[8]

After 1956 Marcel Breuer will hold a large amount of works, mostly for public, governmental or institutional uses. He will further explore the apparent reinforced concrete technology, with cast-in-situ and/or prefabricated structural elements, frequently defining structural facades, always with strong plastic expressiveness. Breuer's experiences conformed an appropriate and timely repertoire of examples, matching the considerable increase of the application of the reinforced/prestressed concrete technology, employing innovative constructive techniques and relying on its plastic and structural qualities – characteristics that became a worldwide architectural and engineering high-tech trend at that moment. Breuer's most promising, visually pleasing and not so difficult to emulate brutalist examples were able to opportunely benefit all architects of that moment, everywhere in the world. In fact, the 1960s-70s decades were flooded by Breuer's-like works, with or without a formal statement or a direct recognition of such affiliation, by their authors.

This very brief account of Breuer's professional career is not meant to exhaust the subject.[9] Its aim is to stress the relevance of his works and their *exemplary* role for at least two different generations of architects – from the anxious modernists[10] of the 1940s-50s to the brutalists experiments of the 1960s-70s.

BACK AND FORTH: SOME CHOSEN SCENARIOS

Breuer's American career displays some interesting elective affinities as well as stimulating and fruitful architectural dialogues among peers, admirers and himself. Such affinities are not at all one-directional, and seem to bounce back and forth, North and South of the continents. As had happened all over the world, Brazilian architects were also aware and fond of Breuer's contributions; on the other hand, Breuer's works seem attentive to Brazilian *carioca* modern architecture and its astounding international breakthrough in the late 1940s.

It is not so difficult a task to follow the trail of clues of Breuer's elective affinities, to identify its footprints and to propose some smart insights on the subject. But it is also not so easy, because this has to be, first and foremost, an essentially visual research. As so, this paper briefness and lack of images will only suggest ideas, without properly exhausting them.

One of the most important conceptual tools to undertake the job is available, although it is not always quite at hand: The dates, that must always be taken in careful consideration, most specially the design dates, instead of the building completion ones. Another conceptual tool is to adopt an attitude of fundamental fondness about the works themselves. Meaning, a wish to approach them with a candid and unbiased regard, stripped off the several layers of previous frozen ideas attached to them along their recent history, disregarding the generic and outdated statements about modern architecture, its works and authors, and trying to consider them inside a broader and global scale vision. It's an attitude born from a profound respect to the documents – i.e., the buildings. And it states a position against the *a priori* concept of cultural transposition that, by definition, pretends that ideas and forms are born elsewhere and then travel along an imaginary, one-way axis, flowing from North to South: A pervasive idea but also, a most inefficient one; that very frequently is hastily invocated and lightly misused to interpret the architectural facts and deeds of the second half of the 20th century modern architecture.

Having in mind such theoretical caveats,[11] one may try on following the proposed trail. The track will look closer at Breuer's revisions of some modern *carioca* milestones and his transmutations of the "V," "Y," "T," "W" columns, shifting from Niemeyer's plasticity to Marcel's structuralism, considering Breuer's light & shadow principles and its incarnation in his molded structural façades. For briefness, this paper will not advance on the collation of important Breuer's works and other architects' variations, which will be explored only for the visual/oral presentation, when it will also be references and hints on other interwoven scenarios of correspondences and interchanges – that as for ever, conform the sheer basis from which good architecture usually flourishes.

As a first step, it is necessary to remember the world-wide impact and deep influence of modern Brazilian architecture outstanding buildings of the 1940s-50s, also heightened by the relative void of other meaningful architectural propositions at that most complicated moment of the immediate post-Second World War, when Europe was destroyed and civil construction in the USA was paralyzed. When the initial positive impression and praising wore out there followed several criticisms, of uneven quality, depth and consistency, and some heated debates in and around architectural events, like the recently created São Paulo Art and Architecture Biennial (1951).

But practicing architects, then as now, only very seldom take their time to write consequential critiques about the works of other architects. Instead, what architects frequently do, albeit often in a quiet and not self-proclaiming way, is to *correct* other authors ideas and redraft them inside their own designs.

'I CAN DO IT MUCH BETTER' WOULD BE A MOST APPROPRIATE 'MOTTO' FOR ARCHITECTS AND DESIGNERS.

And besides, this is how architecture accumulates its disciplinary knowledge: By trial and error, by creating, divulgating, imitating and re-creating.

The need for disciplinary knowledge accumulation and exchange was even more acute at that moment – the 1940s-70s – when modern architecture battles, although proclaiming its victory over academicism, had not at all ceased. On the contrary: Modern architecture disciplinary field was still a *work-in-progress* and having to deal with the troubles and contradictions of its expansion and success. Doctrines do no feed bellies, neither they resolve details. There was a then a strong need to define practical paths for actual design necessities, a situation that stimulated architects into being very conscious of other colleagues' works: Not just by curiosity, but by the necessity of finding support for the development of their own creations.

And although modern architecture was supposedly strictly functional, and so, each design should be born from the scratch and almost *ex-nihilo*, in reality it was really not quite so: Stylistic questions had not stopped to intervene within modern architecture practices, neither its constraints would disappear just because some of its more famous architects and organic critics were nominally against the idea of *style*.[12] At that moment of the middle of 20th century, all architects, more or less famous, more or less creative, were involved in the expansion of the boundaries of their discipline, and committed to the search of adequate proven ideas, materials, detailing and design solutions, able to help to gradually define a suitable repertoire for their own daily use.

So it is not at all impossible that Breuer were aware of modern Brazilian architecture propositions and would like to adapt and *correct* some of Niemeyer's forms for its own use – like the "V" and "W" columns. Niemeyer begins to employ these devices after 1950 in apartment and office towers (i.e., JK Housing Ensemble, Belo Horizonte, 1951; California Building, São Paulo, 1951) and multipurpose pavilions (i.e., the Ibirapuera Park Ensemble, São Paulo, 1951-53), experimenting with the plasticity of reinforced concrete. But at that moment his designs were considered *too fancy*, and Niemeyer's argument about their supposed structural role did not convinced the more puritan critics.[13]

Although Breuer once said that "art is not necessary to make a good building; this is not a time like the Gothic period,"[14] his strict functional position was then already shifting. First he introduces, here and there, a sculptural detail inside some houses, like in fireplaces (Starkey House, Duluth, Minnesota, 1954-55; Gagarin House, Litchfeld, Connecticut, 1954-55); then he experiments with folded and hypar structures (the UNESCO Building auditorium, Paris, 1953-58; Canteen at the Van-Leer

Office Building, Amstelveen, The Netherlands, 1957-58; Hunter College at Bronx, New York, 1955-59). His experiments with the plastic expressivity of concrete structures begin to gain further momentum with his religious buildings (St.John's Abbey and University Complex, 1954-68).

His first and masterful use of "V" columns – revised and *corrected* – appear at the covered cloister walks of the Convent of the Annunciation in Bismarck, North Dakota, 1954-62, which have a most striking visual similarity with the Ibirapuera's Marquise. This is not at all a coincidence; but the differences are also remarkable. The extended sinuous marquise of the Ibirapuera Park has 650 meters in its larger axis, its horizontal slab being supported by 106 cylindrical columns with 50 centimeters of diameter, plus eight "V" columns positioned at its four narrow extremities. The straight regular south walk of the Annunciation Convent has ~ 3,15 meters per 125 meters, with nineteen "V" columns in the external side and fourteen towards the patio. Breuer's regular repetition of the *special* "V" column is perhaps more akin with the porticoed palaces of Brasília, designed by Niemeyer in 1957-59. The Ibirapuera slab has no visible beams, or better, they are enclosed inside the slab depth. At the Convent cloister walks the beams are explicit and combine with the "V" columns to connect each parallel pair; but this is only visible when you walk along it, since the beams are hidden behind the columns, in a frontal view. As so, its slab looks extremely light, as it happens in the Ibirapuera's. Niemeyer's marquise received a smooth finishing and whitewash, while Breuer's cloister's walk is made of exposed concrete; but its light color and the excellent handicraft of the forms give it a marmoreal appearance that it's the opposite of rudeness. The Ibirapuera's columns have neither a base nor a capital, while the Convent's "V" columns are elegantly supported by a thin basis, a cylindrical steel joint apparatus disposed over a low stone wall, as a kind of elevated groundwork. Thanks to that subtleness the "V" columns seem to *float*, when seen from some distance. The game and play of proximities and differences do not stop there, and could keep on with the similarities and differences of measurements, the choice of the floors, and so on. What they do have in common is that both "V" columns are not really *necessary*, from a strict functional point of view, and could be easily substituted by simple columns. Their existence is born from *kunstwollen* and aesthetic considerations,

AND SO THEY FOLLOW ONE OF NIEMEYER'S FAMOUS APHORISMS: "THE FORM THAT CREATES BEAUTY HAS A MOST IMPORTANT FUNCTION IN ARCHITECTURE".[15]

But "VYWT" columns may be designed as to have an effective and irreplaceable structural role. That happens when their capitals are not only an ornament but a device into transferring distributed loads above to a single supporting point bellow – and that is not at all a novelty since this is the factual reason why capitals do exist in construction. Niemeyer's "VW" columns best examples (i.e., The Agricultural Pavilion of the Ibirapuera Park Ensemble, 1953) serve the purpose of diminishing the quantity of columns as to create a freer ground floor. Since it is used in a dom-ino like structure, the building is intended to be as light and transparent as possible; and even when there is the external or internal juxtaposition of louvers or *brise-soleils* at the façades, they are still as light as possible, in a figurative and also, in a literal sense. Breuer's first "V" columns for the UNESCO initial project to the Porte Maillot site followed this same reasoning and pattern and are meant for a light and transparent tower.

That completely changes when Breuer begins to design his façades with prefabricated faceted panels. In a text published in *Architectural Record* in April 1966, Breuer declares:

that sheet of enclosure – that division between indoors and
outdoors, the skin of a building – has again requested new
answers to its problems, which have given a sharp turn to the

course of architecture in recent years. The concept of a large
building, expressed by regularly spaced structural supports and
non-bearing, lightweight separations – including the outside
wall – although logical, has left unanswered some problems of
structure, climate and equipment.[16]

> His answer to these problems was already theoretically debated in his *Sun and Shadow* book, and will be given an integrated solution, combining structure, paneling and sunscreen, with his deep façades of the 1960s-70s.
>
> The use of structural façades claims for a subtle but fundamental structural change: It becomes more convenient to displace the supporting columns to the perimeter, instead of recessed from the plane of the façades. But except in industrial and laboratory buildings, Breuer's use of the prefabricated façade panels occurs only in the elevated floors. Therefore, some kind of structural transition must be proposed as to define a more open, public or civic ground floor. Breuer will then design a variety of transition beams and special-designed columns to solve this conundrum. They go from the massive but elegant solution of the IBM Research Center in La Gaude, Var, France (1960-61) with a combined "Y"/"W" design, where the ground floor is treated almost as if he wanted to maintain the *natural*

topography of the place; to the "T" column of the Technology II Building, New York University Campus, Bronx, New York (1964-69, Meister Hall of Bronx Community College). They admit elegant variations, like the "T" columns of the Engineering and Applied Science Building, Yale University, New Haven (1965-69, Becton Center) and can be adapted to peculiar situations - as in the asymmetric "T" columns of the Office building in Syracuse, New York (1969). In other cases, given a freer situation than that of a heavy façade of a high-rise building, the creative imagination can flow to its limits: As in the superb tree-like with 12 arms internal columns of the Library at St. John Abbey and University, Collegeville, Minnesota (1964-66).

These and other molded façade panels and "VYWT" columns used in several Breuer's works of the 1960-70s configured a highly influential formal and constructive paradigm that resonated through an uncountable number of architects based on every city and continent. As so, Breuer's ideas gained momentum and status, and became the focus of a wide web of elective affinities. That did not happen only for its functional reasons – its capacity of controlling sun and playing with the shadows, or for structural and constructive reasons, or because the possibility of an industrial scale repetition had the potential to promote the industrialization dream that Breuer was looking for since his Bauhaus years. As in the case of any other elective affinity, it's mostly a question of affections and passions. Or, quoting Breuer: "You exploit a structural system with passion as well as logic. [...] Structure is not just a means to a solution. It is also a principle and a passion."[17]

NOTES

EN. Article originally presented at the Seminar "Architectural Elective Affinities: Correspondences, Transfers, Inter/Multidisciplinarity. European Architectural History Network – EAHN," held by FAU USP (March 2013).

1. Myra Warhaftig, *Deutsche judische Architekten vor und nach 1933- Das Lexikon* (Berlin: Reimer, 2005), 95-97. I'm very much obliged to Anat Falbel, who kindly provided me this source of reference.

2. Henri-Russell Hitchcock, *Architecture: Nineteenth and Twentieth Centuries* (New Haven/London: Yale University Press, 1977), 517.

3. Peter Blake, ed., *Marcel Breuer: Sun and Shadow. The Philosophy of an Architect* (London: Longmans/Green and Co, 1956), 141.

4. Ibid.

5. As stated in the MoMA Exhibition History List of the 1940s at http://www.moma.org/learn/resources/archives/archives_exhibition_history_list#1940.

6. Blake, *Marcel Breuer*.

7. Henry Russell Hitchcock, *Built in USA: Post-war Architecture* (New York: Museum of Modern Art, s.d), 15.

8. From year 2000 on, there has been a discreet resurrection of a critical interest in Breuer's works, as in Robert F.Gatje's *memoirs*, the comprehensive catalogue of his works by Isabelle Hyman and some studies on his houses by Antonio Armesto and Joachim Driller. Still, they are mostly focused on his first two phases, and not quite on the brutalist last one.

9. See also Ruth Verde Zein, "Sun, shadow and fan," *Summa+* 120, February 2012, 134-135. A Spanish version can be consulted at: http://revistasummamas.com.ar/revista_pdf/120/16#visor.

10. Sarah Williams Goldhagen and Réjean Legault, *Anxious Modernisms. Experimentation in Postwar Architectural Culture* (Quebec: Canadian Centre for Architecture/MIT, 2000).

11. See the fourth text of this book: "When Documenting Is Not Enought."

12. Sarah Williams Goldhagen, "Something to Talk about: Modernism, Discourse, Style," *Journal of the Society of Architectural Historians* 64/2, June 2005, 144-167, http://www.jstor.org/stable/25068142.

13. Ruth Verde Zein, "Oscar Niemeyer. Da crítica alheia à teoria própria," *Arquitextos* 151.04, Vitruvius, December 2012, http://www.vitruvius.com.br/revistas/read/arquitextos/13.151/4608.

14. Marcel Breuer, *Marcel Breuer, Buildings and Projects 1921-1961* (London: Thames & Hudson, 1962), 181.

15. Oscar Niemeyer, *A forma na arquitetura* (Rio de Janeiro: Avenir, 1978), 54.

16. Marcel Breuer, "The Faceted Molded Façade: Depth, Sun and Shadow," *Architectural Record*, April 1966, 171. Republished in Marcel Breuer, *Nuevas Construcciones y Proyectos* (Barcelona: Gustavo Gili, 1970), 13.

17. Breuer, *Marcel Breuer*, 19.

HARD CASES

**BRICKS AND BRUTS
FROM NORTH AND SOUTH**

BRUTALISM IS BEING RECONSIDERED IN CONTEMPORARY DEBATES AND PUBLICATIONS. NEW APPROACHES ARE BEING PROPOSED, GOING BEYOND THE PREJUDICES AND ALMOST OBLIVION OF THE TERM AND ITS MANIFESTATIONS IN THE LAST DECADES OF THE 20TH CENTURY. NEW PANORAMIC OVERVIEWS AND DEEP STUDY CASES ARE BEING PROPOSED, EXPANDING ITS UNDERSTANDING. BUT ALTHOUGH IT IS EASY TO PERCEIVE WHAT THE SUBJECT WE HAVE AT hand is, it is still complicate to try and define the term and what it stands for.[1] A broad international research on its manifestations would find a complex web of multiple and varied descriptions, spread along a six decades' timeline, each speaking from a slightly different position. Some of these are partial recurrences and patched retellings, adjusted to attend to different interests and sets of buildings, not always with the same quality and consistency – not being rare to find nonsensical, biased and out-of-date samples. It may be argued[2] that the tag brutalism does not support an essentialist definition, being indissolubly bound to a set of complex historical circumstances, which are not restricted to a single place, time, creator or commentator.

Among scholars, it is usual to try and surpass such conundrum going back to brutalism supposed origins; the most preferred chosen ones being Le Corbusier's post-Second World War works and Banham's 1950s-60s reports on the British new brutalism case. Although comforting and apparently grounded, such effort of validating a definition by leaning on the force of the past authorities is also problematic. The rereading of the *first ones*, be it in a straight literal or in more fancy and interpretative ways, is bound, in the best cases, to open up new possibilities without really closing them; in the worst cases, to dully repeat some old misunderstandings. Every other definition of brutalism and what it entitles will probably not arrive at an indisputable and stable explanation. There is not, there has never been and there would never be a way to assert an untainted, a-ideological discourse on brutalism.

But although it is extremely complicated to pinpoint its precise definition, there is definitely a pervading mood that connects the so-called brutalist buildings. Like, a certain fondness for exploring the plastic expression of structural solutions and the inherent qualities of each material employed – a trait often interpreted as a desire to express a moral and material truth. However, the sheer complexity of the aesthetic and material operations involved in the design and construction of its best examples, exceeds by far a single ethical premise.

HAVING SAID THIS, THE PRESENT ARTICLE IS NOT ABOUT FINDING A CONCLUSIVE DEFINITION OF 'BRICK BRUTALISM'.

The name has been applied to brick structures of the 1950-60s, either of homogeneous fabric or interspersed with concrete, steel or wood frames. When considering each building, the existence of a brick brutalism is easily prone to doubts on its dependability, for their specificities, differences in attitude

HARD CASES

and results are as striking as their visual proximities. However, this article does not propose to radically question brick brutalism existence. Here the label, and the works it was applied to, is accepted as a historical fact, inasmuch as some canonical authors did use it to explain or debate some connections among those buildings. As they are remarkable pieces of architecture, they would live quite well without ever being attached to the label. Still, they have been circumstantially referred to as brutalist, and that would serve us as enough proof of the existence of *brick bruts*; and to ground some extrapolation, naming as so other analogous examples, designed and constructed simultaneously, elsewhere, by else whom.

Nevertheless, the brick brut label will remain a most problematic subject. To accept it *ad hoc* may be a superficial assumption; to extend its use to other examples, a superficial attempt. But surfaces, and their detailed consideration, are not unimportant features when considering architecture, its characteristics and meanings. It is probably worth the effort "recognizing the problematic of appearance," as stated by Leatherbarrow and Mostafavi. The more so, as it depends to be put forward on a careful consideration of "the correlation between its processes of construction and its appearance."[3]

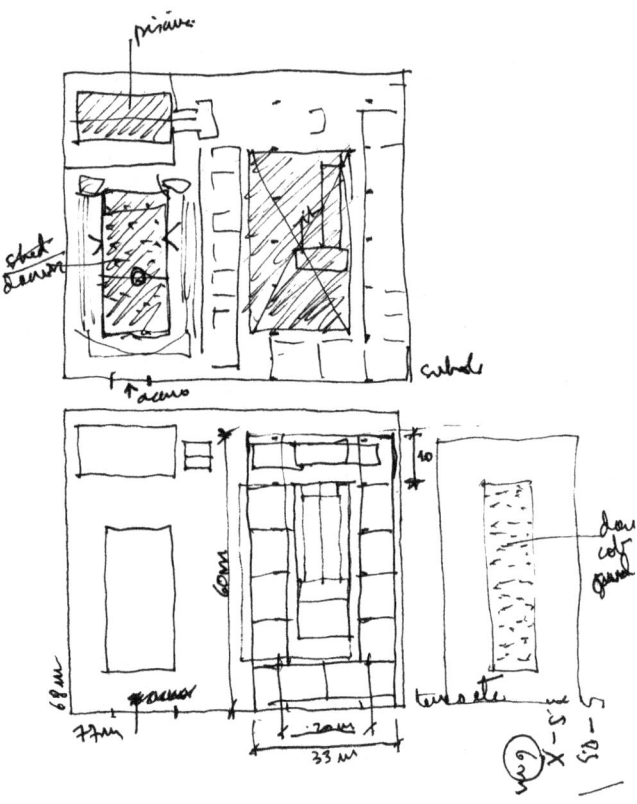

12 de Outubro School, plans of the acess level, social area, classroom level and covering, São Paulo SP. Vilanova Artigas, 1962. Drawing Ruth Verde Zein

'AS FOUND:' LITERAL, ALLEGORIC, PRAGMATIC

Considering the vague words so often used in architectural writings, Rowe and Slutzky pointed that "it may indeed be futile to attempt to make efficient critical instruments of such approximate definitions; perhaps, any such attempt can only result in sophistries."[4] The notion of *as found*, as exposed by Banham[5] in connection with brutalism, may be arguably included in the list of sophisms and long-range metaphors, so often ingrained in architectural critiques. And yet, Rowe and Slutzky believe that a further examination of such imprecise terms may eventually reveal a "lucid complexity," and to expose some interesting levels of meanings.

Except at the mythical primitive hut or when erecting a most improvised shelter, constructive materials are not used *as found*: To properly build, some degree of transformation of the natural resources is always necessary. So, when in 1955 Banham summarizes "the qualities of that object" (the Hunstanton School by Allison and Peter Smithson) in three points, the last one – "the valuation of materials for the inherent qualities *as found*"[6] – should not be taken by the letter, but as an allegory. Here, as in his many other writings, Banham's interpretations are complex, with several layers of clear and hidden agendas and filled with analogies with other architectural and artistic debates. Further along, as his *as found* allegory still looks like too weak or unclear, Banham proposes its precision by using another, also vague, expression, *an image*: "The building should be an immediately apprehensive visual entity, and the form grasped by the eye should be confirmed by experience of the building in use."[7] Acting as a *maquis* with a loose cannon, he profusely extends the allegories by also proposing that new brutalism was somewhat interested (or so he believes) in the subtle slithering from visual to sensorial; from the classical definition of beauty by Thomas Aquinas as "that which seen, pleases" to a more forceful *sublime* definition of beauty, as primarily affecting emotions (possibly not so pleasing to the eye). In the article's final words Banham remembers that "materials *as found* are raw materials,"[8] only to connect them again with *emotions*, by quoting Le Corbusier's famous 1920s aphorism *"L'Architecture c'est, avec des matières bruts*, établir *des rapports* émouvants;"[9] which he believes would be more appropriate to "our time, and not his."[10]

Although the *as found* allegory was proposed à *propos* of Hunstanton's exposed materials, in his 1966 book Banham admits that the connection between bricks and brutalism was established by the Maisons Jaoul (1951).[11] He is aware that the label brutalism may not be easily applied to Jaoul's or other

HARD CASES

previous buildings by Le Corbusier since the 1935 Petit Maison de Weekend. But he realizes – now from his mid-1960s point of view – that "brutalism, as a going style, proved to be largely a matter of surfaces derived from Jaoul."[12] Anyway, he considers that "the use of Jaoul's crude and primitivistic building techniques in Europe was a shock to sophisticated constructional habits;" and mentions James Stirling's remark: "The labour that built them 'with ladders, hammers and nails' was algerian."[13]

RECENT STUDIES TEND TO ACCEPT THE SUPPOSED 'PRIMITIVENESS' OF THE BRUTALIST BUILDINGS (CONCRETE OR BRICK) NOT AS A REGRESSION OF CONSTRUCTIVE METHODS BUT AS AN AESTHETICAL CHOICE.

Von Moos emphasizes the material crudeness as an attitude of bold audacity and connection with the origins: *"La nostalgie des ruines, de la brique nue, de la pierre non taillé, du béton brut et the l'héroïsme dur des débuts que l'on trouve sur les chantier des constructions."*[14] For him, in the half-destroyed Europe of the immediate post-Second World War, rough bricks and badly executed concrete denoted a resurgence of the romantic theme of the ruins.

Under that moment's difficult circumstances, Stirling's (via Banham's) remarks on Jaoul's – as a shock to established constructive habits – is perhaps less an accurate and experienced analysis than a juvenile critique. On the other hand, Stirling & Gowan's actual reaction to Jaoul's is not a remark but a building: Ham Common Flats (1955-58). The neat finishing of its brick walls may be interpreted as a magisterial *correction*, from a disciple, condescendingly showing off to the masters how things should be *properly done*, with the same scarce resources. These fixing and emending attitudes pervades that generation and appears at other brick brutalism examples, whose connection with Jaoul's might not have meant by their authors, as imitations, but as smart counterpoint replications.

Anyway, the effort to make the best of hard circumstances is possibly a more realistic motive for the use of exposed bricks and rough concrete in the immediate post-Second World War. Accordingly, the *as found* characteristic pointed by Banham may accept a pragmatic interpretation: While it is not possible, in architecture, to use materials as *objets trouvés* (as in painting or sculpture), it is simply easier, quicker and cheaper to propose as minimum transformative processes as possible – as long as the results satisfy the needs and requirements of that moment.

HARD CASES

BUILDERS, ENGINEERS, ARCHITECTS

Keeping on the same track – that architecture is not just a thing in itself, but a means to serve human needs by transforming the environment with the scarce resources at hand – one may open up other paths. The influence of clients and the professional contribution of builders and engineers in the decision-making process of architectural design and outputs are often minimized in architectural discourses. But there are several authors that do mind the subject,[15] giving interesting clues to further examine the subject at hand.

After Second World War, there is an important growth on the use of reinforced and post-tensed concrete to build infrastructural equipment (dams, bridges etc.); around 1952-53 such know-how was becoming available to everyday architectural uses, all over the world. Albeit in the 1920s, modern architecture masters praised engineers' aesthetics as a stimuli to achieve a desired architectural renovation, in their works that aim was frequently restricted to a visual approach, rather than to an actual structural and constructive transformation.[16] That will radically and massively change from the 1950s, when a happy new connubiality between architects, engineers and builders becomes possible. Brutalism, as a characteristic architectural trend of that moment, is its most obvious outcome.

As so, the image of 1950s-60s brutalism may derive from the quest of the sublime instead of classical beauty; the search of primitivism and craving for the origins; or, the use of exposed bricks and concrete may be a recurrence of the romantic longing for ruins, accentuated by the presence of post-war debris. But it may also, and with the same importance, be derived from the fact that engineers, builders and architects were then – not only in Europe, but everywhere – speaking the same language. Textually, visually and constructively they were sharing the same progressive eagerness towards structural bold audacity, obtained by the clever, rational use of simple materials. They were resolutely trying to make the best out of minimum resources, elevating the *ad hoc* necessities into a kind of *moral standard*, from which they expected to derive their design and building processes.

In the case of the *brick bruts* something similar may have also happened. Le Corbusier's Jaoul's is as much a quest for appearance, texture and tactility as it is a clever choice, in the face of restricted construction site resources, of downsizing the expected quality of the building finishing – here thus exploring its *as found* or *primitivistic* aspects. Other *brick bruts* could have been interested in exploring other paths. Some of them may have even tried to bring forth an opposite attitude, as their design seemed to be aimed at the feasibility of using bricks, not as a link to the past, but in different, new and innovative ways.

TWO ANTIPODE HARD BRICK BRUT CASES

Although the number of *brick brut* examples exceeded by far rough concrete ones in England in the 1950s, in his 1966 book Banham prefers to include his local bricks in the *main course* and to collect non-English examples to debate the "hard cases of brick brutalism."[17] He states that "the hardest case" and "certainly the most enigmatic is Sigurd Lewerentz's Markuskyrka outside Stockholm,"[18] Sweden (1956-64), and that "many of these hard cases are churches;" including, as examples, Figini and Pollini's Santa Maria dei Poveri, Milan, Italy (1952-54) and Van der Broeck and Bakema church at Nagele, Holland (1958-62). Considering these *brick brut* examples one may also include in the list a most interesting and precocious example: The Church of Christ Worker at Atlantida (1952-59), Uruguay, by Eladio Dieste. As these buildings have been thoroughly studied by many authors, they will be here examined exclusively under the issue of the brick brutalism. For the sake of brevity, only to extreme cases – geographically speaking – will be further considered.

Sigurd Lewerentz (1887-1965) belongs to the same generations as Le Corbusier's, and begins his professional life as mechanical engineer, before training as an architect. His Markus Church is a mature work with a most innovative attitude in the overall design and detailing. Eladio Dieste's (1917-2000) Church of Christ Worker is an almost maiden project designed and executed by a young engineer, builder and professor of large structures. Both were personally involved in religious matters, and saw no contradiction between the search of aesthetical pleasure and the design of exquisite sacred spaces. Both cases are parish churches: Traditionally, a most economical construction with restricted resources, managed to obtain cost-effective performance and maximum results, and meant to last: They are not supposed to be cheap, but durable and easy to maintain.

In both cases the eye is attracted, in the exteriors, by the continuous brick fabric and the vertical planes that enclose the buildings; and in the interiors, by the soft sombre lightning and the amazingly suave curves of the roofs and walls. There is no concrete to be seen: It is discreetly used in the Swedish case and completely absent in the Uruguayan example. Whereas the northern reformed church is asymmetrical in plan and elevations, the southern catholic church is strikingly symmetrical. The Swedish church has two naves, a main one to the south and a secondary one to the north; the Uruguayan has a single nave. Both have a bell tower: Attached to the other parish facilities in the Markus Church, and freely standing at the Christ Worker's. Their overall dimensions are quite similar: The Uruguayan's single nave has a striking transversal span (as said, with no concrete at all), while the Swedish's double nave is arranged with a liberally open, almost transparent connection between the two aisles.

The curves of walls and roofs are not randomly disposed, but result from cleverly designed forms, aimed to simultaneously contain and buttress the structures. This occurs in a more thoroughly symmetrical and didactic way in Atlántida. There, hollowed ceramic bricks are used to design the roof as a single surface, alternating curved and plain planes; a trait that reverberates in the walls, born from straight foundations and progressively waving as they raise to stitch with the roof's sinusoidal pace. In Stockholm, the need to buttress the transversal span is solved in a more subtle, asymmetrical way: In the south side, by the slight waving of the common brick wall, in the north, propped by the second nave span.

The ingenuity of both solutions shows that Lewerentz and Dieste had elaborate skills as architects, engineers and builders. They did know how to take full advantage of rational calculus to achieve singular but simple results, within the limitations and possibilities of traditional materials and under innovative construction methods. Most probably they both believed, following Aquinas words, in beauty as the splendour of truth.

INNOVATIVE BRICK BRUTALISM

Any brick building benefits from the traditional meanings associated with the material (earthliness, warmth, tactility, local identity). But that is not necessarily the 1950s-60s *brick bruts* only or main concern. The circumstances of place, author, client, availability of materials, and professional expertise provided other aesthetical, constructive and architectural opportunities.

The *brick bruts* examples here discussed crave to promote, with bricks, a confluence between rational thinking and creative forms. These two churches by Lewerentz and Dieste display a clever performance uniting state-of-the art calculus and structurally adequate, daring forms.

THEIR INNOVATIVE MOOD WAS ASSOCIATED WITH THE USE OF A MOST TRADITIONAL MATERIAL, FAMILIAR TO CLIENTS, BUILDERS AND WORKERS, PERMITTING AN EASIER AND COST-EFFECTIVE CONSTRUCTIVE PROCESS.

HARD CASES

Finally, these 1950s examples may be connected with brutalism not just for their rough brick appearance or by some rather imprecise relationship with a vague idea of *as found*; nor are they *primitivistic*. On the contrary, they are very sophisticated and complex design propositions. They may be called brutalist mostly by the fact that they share, with other brick and non-brick brutalist buildings, the same fondness of expressing innovative structural solutions, adequate to a given constructive material. Even if, in the case of *brick bruts*, it is a most traditional one.

Their attitude – of achieving beauty through innovation, by considering the complexities of the rational thinking – is perhaps, one of the most appealing features of the best brutalist buildings. A trait that is still strong enough, and perhaps, fruitful enough, to keep on attracting new generations of architects and critics from another century.

NOTES

EN. Article previously published at: Horacio Torrent, ed., "El Desafio del Tiempo. Proyecto y Persistencia del Patrimonio Moderno," *Anais do DOCOMOMO Chile*, Santiago do Chile, 2014, 33-40. English version originally presented at the European Architectural History Network – EAHN Conference (Turim, July 2014).

1. Ruth Verde Zein, "Brutalist Connections: What it Stands for," *10º Seminário DOCOMOMO Brasil* (Curitiba: DOCOMOMO, 2013), http://www.xdocomomobrasil.com.br/download/artigos/conexoes/CON_49.pdf.

2. See the tenth text of this book: "Modern Tradition and Contemporary Culture. The Contribution of the 1950s-70s Brutalism in Brazil and Elsewhere."

3. David Leatherbarrow and Mohsen Mostafavi, *Surface Architecture* (Cambridge: MIT, 2002), 2.

4. Collin Rowe and Robert Slutsky, "Transparency: Literal and phenomenal," in: Collin Rowe, *The Mathematics of the ideal Villa and other essays* (Cambridge: MIT, 1982), 160.

5. Reyner Banham, "The New Brutalism," *Architectural Review* 708, 1955, 857.

6. Ibid, 857.

7. Ibid, 858.

8. Ibid, 861.

9. "Architecture is, through raw materials, to express emotional relations." Free translation.

10. Banham, "The New Brutalism," 861.

11. Reyner Banham, *The New Brutalism. Ethic or Aesthetic?* (London: Architectural Press, 1966), 125.

12. Ibid., 85.

13. Ibid., 86.

HARD CASES

14. "A ruin nostalgia, of bare bricks, uncut stones, rough concrete and pure heroism of the beginnings found on this works." Free translation. Stanislaus Von Moos, "L'Europe après la pluie ou le brutalism face a l'Histoire," in: *Le Corbusier et la question du brutalisme*, ed. Jacques Sbriglio (Paris: Parenthèses, 2013), 65.

15. As for example, Philippe Potié's on Le Corbusier's La Tourette Covent. Philippe Potié, *The Monastery of Saint Marie de la Tourette* (Paris: Foundation Le Corbusier, 2001), 80.

16. Rather, numerous works of the 1920-30s modernist canon are still built and structured in a very traditional way, prevailing the unifying white painted plaster as a resource to ensure a modern image.

17. Banham, *The New Brutalism*, 125-127.

18. Ibid., 125.

| BR | LATIN AMERICA: | CRITICAL |
| 5 | THOUGHTS | READINGS |

NULLA DIE SINE LINEA

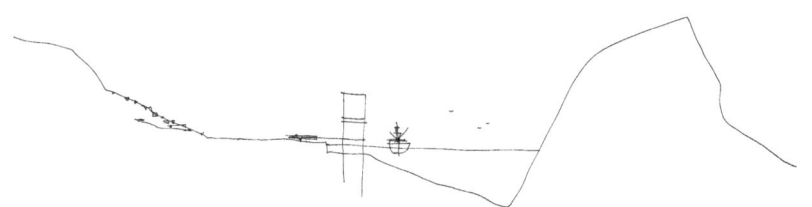

Vitória Bay, section, Vitória ES. Paulo Mendes da Rocha, 1993.
Paulo Mendes da Rocha Archive

For some people drawing is like breathing. There are others who fight hard to achieve the spontaneity of drawing. Then there are the rest of us. Whatever: Once there is a drawing or a sketch, either if it is an accomplished fact or an imperfect deed, it is also, always, a thing in itself. The traces of its production fade, and the object gives out its infinite finitude.

It was an ordinary day in 1997. Architect Paulo Mendes da Rocha sits before a large thick white, double-format, 30 x 60 cm sheet of paper and gets ready to do the drawing I had asked him to. That drawing would conclude the job I was undertaking, at his request, to prepare his application documents to compete for a full professorship at the University of São Paulo's School of Architecture and Urbanism. He takes the pen and with a single gesture he draws it all – mountain, city, port, sea, building, boat, canal, mountain, valley. The line is almost a Steinberg's, the pen hardly raises from the paper.

The composition is balanced and has a surprisingly diagonal symmetry: The line of the territory could almost be superposed to Caravaggio's *The Entombment of Christ*, with his head to the left, lower than the top of his knees to the right. Or, in a less dramatic and closer image, the topographic line retraces Charlotte Perriand's profile while lying on the 1928's chaise lounge she designed, and Le Corbusier named. However, the center of the drawing is not the landscape, but the artificial and straight architecture lines. Just two vertical strokes, raised very high by the subtle contrast with the topography, drawn top-bottom until they dig in the mud; and only four other horizontal lines to define a roof garden, an intermediate belvedere floor, and a pier ground floor placed above water and tides, connecting with the city. Three birds observe the scene hovering above boats and architecture – they may be *Sterna hirundinacea*, or *South American Terns*, commonplace birds in the Victoria Bay area, in the state of Espírito Santo, Brazil.

On the landside, a horizontal building anchors the tower by leaning on a single point, just like a wading-bird at rest, accommodating the utilities the city provides and the residues the city will process. In close detail, one sees other artificial lines: Where the landscape was transformed to create the pier's floor there is the vertical retaining-wall that guarantees the draft and the artificial horizontal bottom line that was gained by the dredging works; the three lines that allow the existence of the sea harbor. The only natural horizontal straight line in the drawing, and in life, is that of the water: A mineral liquid material that challenges, with its apparently straight surface, as seen from limited human eyes, the curvature of the universe.

NULLA DIE

SINE LINEA

It is a deliberate sketch, a compact and concise synthesis. It does not overvalue the romantic fetish of the allegedly spontaneous creation. On the contrary, here art and architecture are assumed and presented as shameless artifices. Economy of means have not came easily and it is proudly and rightfully displayed. Children mess before learning to eat by their mouths, extended oral discourses barely explain what poetry reveals in just a few words. The struggle with words never finishes, but it temporarily ends at the break of a new dawn, as in Drummond.

This sketch recalls the wisdom of a Shodo calligrapher master, tracing with his brush a perfect Kanji in just three seconds, that contain thirty-years. A dense and complex simplicity that speaks without words, but that words may help to fully appreciate. Especially if the words are few and brief and happen only because paying homage is in order.

NOTA

EN. Article previously published at: Ruth Verde Zein, "Nulla die sine linea," in: *Paulo Mendes da Rocha, Entre Ideas y Dibujos*, ed. Julio Arroyo (Santa Fé: Unil, 2015), 70-73. Translated by Anita Di Marco and Ann Puntch.

BRENNAND CHAPEL

**A PLACE, THREE WALLS, A FLOOR,
A ROOF AND SOME DETAILS**

THE APPROACH IS THROUGH THE WOODS AND ALONG A SET OF BRICK SHEDS. THE CHAPEL IS FURTHER DOWN, AND ALTHOUGH IT IS WHITE IT DOES NOT IMMEDIATELY STAND OUT AGAINST THE NEARBY EXUBERANT VEGETATION, AND ONLY REVEALS ITSELF AT THE LAST MOMENT. THE CONSTRUCTION HAS A RECTANGULAR PROPORTION OF APPROXIMATELY 2:1 AND ITS LONGITUDINAL AXIS IS ROTATED 15° COUNTERCLOCKWISE FROM THE NORTH.

A concrete pavement establishes a perfectly flat territory, just above the natural ground on the North and East sides. The natural slope to the South and West quadrants discreetly gives notice of a concrete basement, partially clad in stone. There the concrete pavement is above a livable underground, subtly announced by the irregularity of the pavement perimeter on the South side and by an almost imperceptible ventilation slot.

On the Eastern side of the concrete pavement there is a series of rectangular walls positioned in concentric rings. The first rectangular ring of walls has an incomplete perimeter, being defined by its four corners, like a set of frame brackets; each one including a sequence of two or three arches, summing up eleven complete and eight incomplete arches. Its height is similar to the second ring doors' height.

The second rectangular ring of walls is cladded and whitewashed on the outside, but it reveals the thick stone masonry on the inside. It is perforated by twenty arched French-windows, three on each smaller facade, and seven on the larger ones, summing up nineteen tall and narrow arches plus one lower and wider; the stone doorposts provide an old-fashioned appearance. Interior access is possible through some, but not all of these doors.

The third and inner rectangular ring of walls is defined by a sequence of connected transparent glass panels, with no frames, zigzagging for a better support. They are fixed on the ground and structured by corner pieces, and they define a short convex recess, or narthex, on the Northern facade – the chapel's main entrance – with a slight lower height due to the positioning of the upper choir. This is defined by a single concrete beam supported by the first column and supporting a balcony, which is accessible through some stairs placed between the second and the third rings, and between the second and the third arch span of the Western side. Two other accesses, facing each other in the middle portion of the larger sides, discontinue the glass wall; but they were not open on the day I visited the chapel.

A concrete slab roof has the same surface dimension of the second ring of walls, without touching it, apparently floating a little above it, allowing the construction to breathe. The covering slab rests on a longitudinal beam, of trapezoidal section, arranged along the central axis, unloading onto two cylindrical columns, recessed from the edges of the slab and spaced in a 1-4-1 ratio. It is transversely locked by a gutter-beam placed on the central portion of the East side and connecting to the bell tower, which acts as a third external column.

The isolated bell tower, of rectangular plan and hollowed design, like an upright gutter-beam, is placed outside the three concentric rings of walls, stretching beyond and below ground level, defining a potential cascade to capture and storage the rainwater in an underground cistern. On the opposite facade a small and square table/altar balances the composition and prevents the unimpeded approach to the sector that houses the stairs to the choir.

After entering, beyond the narthex and the choir there is the void/nave, and in the other end, the altar/pulpit; to its right, at the Southeast side, there is a narrow flight of stairs accessing the basement. The first column and the balcony choir partially hinder the views to the internal and relatively small spaces – in a similar, but less effectively way, to that of the Saint Peter's Chapel in Campos do Jordão, designed by the same architect.

The unobtrusive basement, barely seen from the outside or noticed from the inside, is accessed through a stair arranged along a broken line path, followed by a narrow aisle going beyond the perimeter of the rectangular ring of walls. Then it broadens into a small cellar/sacristy, wrapped by a stone-clad wall, dimly lit by the narrow window between the concrete and the earth pavements above.

Back in the chapel above, it is possible to notice a variety of details, that abound without becoming excessive: Finishing plates, commemorative plaques, inlaid ceramic pieces, bas-relief drawings and writings on the floors and balcony, bordering the pulpit and the choir. Plus some portable pieces, benches made by folded sheets of iron, wooden seats, backs, and oratories, high standing candle-holders, some statuary standing or fixed, a three-stone-pieced altar; and many other little things, just because God is also in the details.

Natural light comes in filtered; artificial light, unnecessary during the day, is almost industrially arranged in small inlets in the roof slab; the artificial shadows and the natural breeze could soften the constant heat of the climate – but the glasses that preserve also retain, especially when they are left unopened. At first glance it is not pleasing: The fractured arches define a first intriguing barrier, the access by the front and right/West sides enforces the idea of an isolated object, the circumvention to acquire its necessary recognition is not favored by the slope and the trees around it.

But I surround it, walk in, leave, go back, look again and I observe, with the eyes of the skin. I refuse to think on anything before I feel what in fact it is. It is only after getting inside the second ring of walls that my gaze halts and relaxes: What prevails here is the architect's will. A purist white stands out on the outside, but inside the attention is attracted by the relatively richness of details, magnified by the mutable character of the glasses, multiplying transparencies and reflexes. All that without confounding the sight as the color palette is discreet, going from the dark orange of stones and woods to the bluish grey of concrete and ceramics, with hardly any vibrant tone.

Despite being small and discreet, it is not an easy work to understand, let alone to digest. To fully appreciate it, as it deserves, the observer is asked to withhold judgment and proceed into a careful approach, with painstaking attention to every detail. As always – but most especially here – to describe it is not a superfluous task, but a basic and fundamental step.

Most especially when we know that the author is Paulo Mendes da Rocha: It is a great temptation to just forget the building itself and to comment about the author's persona. Even bigger is the temptation to try and explain the work by metaphors, emulating what it is not, instead of appreciating its tectonics, proportion, voids, and materials.

The description here proposed is not absolute, but experiential. Perhaps, almost phenomenological. And now I will allow myself to add to this bare description just a final and single analogy, or poetic license. Walking thought reminded me of how to appreciate a good wine. Instead of assuming the taste will be good just because you read the label, you had better open and enjoy it, thus activating other senses and perceptions: Smell, color, consistency, touch, and then again, the sight. In this case, it's a wine made of a mixture of grape stains, an alchemy of rustic and sophisticated origins, aged in body and young in spirit. It needs to rest to be fully appreciated.

NOTE

EN. Article previously published at: Ruth Verde Zein, "Capilla Brennand: Un Lugar, Tres Muros, un Piso, una Cubierta y unos Detalles." *En Blanco* 1, 2014, 72-73.

MODERN TRADITION AND CONTEMPORARY CULTURE

THE CONTRIBUTION OF THE 1950S-70S BRUTALISM IN BRAZIL AND ELSEWHERE

IN HIS 1941 BOOK 'SPACE, TIME AND ARCHITECTURE. THE GROWTH OF A NEW TRADITION,'[1] HISTORIAN AND ARCHITECTURAL CRITIC SIEGFRIED GIEDION SUGGESTS THAT AFTER OVERCOMING ITS INITIAL AVANT-GARDE DISRUPTIVE MOMENT, MODERNITY WOULD GRADUALLY ESTABLISH ITSELF AS ANOTHER architectural tradition, the tradition of our times. It was a far-fetched affirmation at that early moment, which yet would be proven true in the following years, and perhaps more so far away from his European home. And certainly, the high quality of modern Brazilian architecture that was sprouting at that mid-20th century moment, and internationally celebrated on publications and exhibitions after 1943, assumed then a very precocious role in the construction and reiteration of such new tradition.

From then on – and despite the proclaimed crisis of modernity – it is reasonable to affirm that it is still over the basis of such *modern tradition*, that contemporary architecture rests. For sure, the critical revisions put forward in the last quarter of the 20th century had helped to broaden and re-signify the meaning of a modern tradition. Nowadays it can be perceived not as an exclusively European or North/Western acquisition, but as multiple, diversified, non-linear and complex global arena, stricken by differential densities and paradoxical contradictions, highlighted by many personages and scenarios, and including a large array of contributions, coming from many places and cultures.

The same expansion of the field also applies to Brazil: In recent decades, inside and outside the country, there have been many efforts to broaden the perception of the local contribution to the constitution of a modern tradition. And alongside the necessary revaluation and revalorization of our classical modernity of the 1930-60 period, there have also been increasing numbers of studies and researches widening the field, as to comprise also other important trends and currents occurring in the second half of the 20th century to-day. It is a wide effort, put forward with the help of many hands and still under development.

From the 1940s until the 1960s Brazilian modern architecture was widely published in journals all over the world, but until the 1970s there were very few books proposing a comprehensive overview on Brazilian modern architecture, with the exception of some 1940s and 1950s international exhibitions catalogues – which, by definition, were not meant to give a complete synopsis on the subject as they were designed to divulge some specific contributions. After the inauguration of Brasília (1960) there happens an abrupt decrease in the international interest on the whereabouts of Brazilian architecture; and up to the end of the 20th century almost nothing else was known outside the country about modern and contemporary Brazilian architecture. As so, the common perception about modern Brazilian architecture was still chained to those mid-century praises and detractions that were mostly misinformed and by then, quickly becoming outdated.

The panorama begins to change inside Brazil after the 1980s, with the flourishing of several local periodical publications and the increasing in historical researches led by a younger generation of local critics and scholars, producing a wide variety of critical revisions. Those followed roughly a three-fold path: a) precisions and revisions of the *old sayings* about the heroic modernist moment before Brasília; b) concerted surveys on Brazilian recent architecture, with an interest in its formal, regional and material variety; and finally, some of us (including this author's works strived to: c) proposing alternative ways to reread 20th century Brazilian architectural panorama, overcoming the emphasis on isolated genius or heroes – that almost exclusive marked the Brazilian's architecture historiography until then – to highlighting its complex and multi-layered processes. Which certainly also included the analysis of its best works and architects, but was also aware of Brazilian modern architecture multiple connections with the international disciplinary culture, in a complex to and from movement. Anyway, those three paths are not isolated but connected and consociated in a collective effort aimed to better understand Brazilian's architecture modern tradition – in a broadened and updated sense – as a valuable and multifarious heritage: not as a past achievement, but as a most significant livened legacy with notable and visible effects in the Brazilian's architecture contemporary realm.

That modern architecture several trends and contributions are a livened heritage that is helping the construction of contemporary

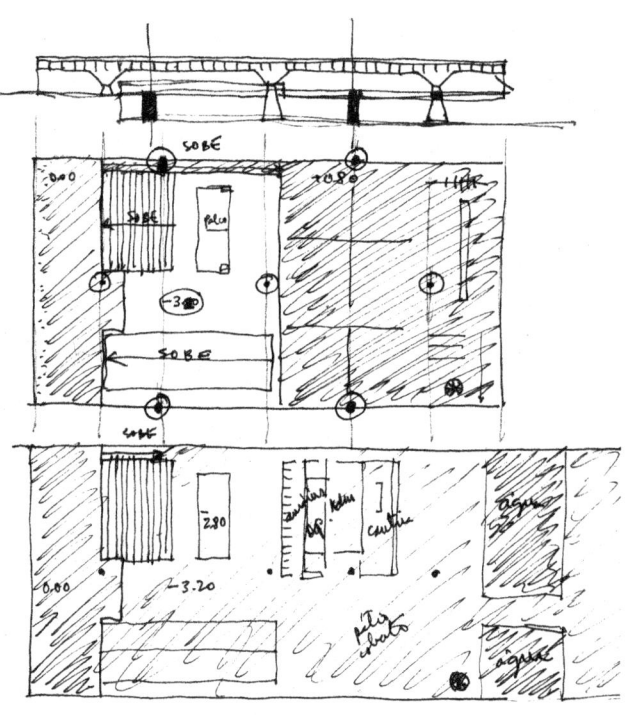

Jardim Calux Center for Child Education, longitudinal section, ground floor and first floor plans, São Bernardo do Campo SP. Paulo Mendes da Rocha, 1972. Drawing Ruth Verde Zein

architecture is a statement that is possibly valid not only in Brazil but also elsewhere; for at least in Latin America, and maybe elsewhere, the modern tradition renovates modernism and makes its contribution be recognized not as a past and closed situation but a present living and complex tradition. Modern ideas, discourses, aspirations and forms, more or less transformed but still strong enough, stand even nowadays at the conceptual core of most of our contemporary architectural debates and propositions, conforming a *lead* that weaves the 21st century architectural scenario – sometimes only weakly disguised by new superficial and brilliant cloaks.

In recent decades, there is again an international increasing interest in Brazilian recent architecture followed, as an almost mandatory counterpoint, by some tentative revaluations of its *golden* past.[2] Some international publications are again displaying clipped selections of Brazil's contemporary architecture, often introduced by critical articles of varied consistency, sometimes written by second-hand *specialists* that hastily try to make heads and tails from Brazil's 8.5 million square kilometers territory and eight prolific decades of modern architecture. That is of course neither an easy nor a simple task; and any instantly cooked answers that intend to solve the query would be necessarily incomplete.[3]

Such recent accounts trying to simplify that complex panorama into some quick and easy explanations are often suggesting the existence of a paradoxical tight combination of bad politics and good geniality as the *causes* of Brazilian modern architecture glory and supposed decay – a most unbelievable and weak explanation. The geniuses hypothesis[4] tries to supplant the gaps and voids from the 1960s to-day by adding a restricted list of new gifted architects to the old consecrated and not-so new ones, from Oscar Niemeyer to Vilanova Artigas and so forth. But even accepting the unavoidable necessity to include the high quality woks of our local best architects' contributions, such simplification – that equals a huge country immense architectural scenario to a restricted group of names – mostly ignores the complexity, the ample variety of contributions it contains. The political hypothesis proposes the existence of a closed connection between the ups and downs of Brazilian modern architecture trends and the country politics, suggesting that its supposed decadence was a direct consequence of the unfortunate military rule that overwhelmed the country on the 1960s-80s. But again, this is just an oversimplification that only blurs the panorama, does not recognize that Architecture has its own disciplinary specificities and ignores the factual historicity. As for example,[5] it is simple to show how some of the best and the strongest experimental Brazilian modern architectures of the 1950-70 were proposed, before and after the military dictatorship, without noticeable aesthetical or conceptual changes; or that quite the same aesthetical trends were being followed all over the world by uncountable other architects on the same decades, who were working inside a large variety of different and sometimes opposite political, economical and cultural situations. A piece of information that, by itself, questions any simple politics-architecture cause-effect simplified hypothesis.

This article does not follow the same paths: it tries not to reinforce old myths with new guises; it does not propose a broad, but also superficial, panoramic overview on Brazilian modern architecture,[6] and it does not display a properly digested but falsely exhaustive list of Brazilian's *exceptional* modern architects and works. It does not contribute with a compact overview, but aims to further analyze, in a more precise and limited way, a precise but somewhat ample historical moment, and inside it, a somewhat restricted, but still very important stylistic tendency. Its concern is aimed to revise a significant and bold trend that flourished, not only in Brazil but also everywhere: The so-called brutalism of the 1950s-70s.

The author's recent researches[7] support the hypothesis that the mid-20th century brutalism was a very important trend not only in Brazil but also all over the world; and that is perhaps even truer in the non-Western countries. And it believes that a further study on the brutalist trend works – considering as conceptual basis the Brazilian case, and most specially, São Paulo's – can be of interest not only in itself, but also, as a first step to develop broader studies aimed to better understand that moment; and, last but not least, that such studies may be able to cast another light on contemporary Brazilian and international *neo-modern* or *neo-brutalist* architecture led by a young generation of architects spread all over the world.

REVISING THE IMPRECISE CHARACTERIZATION OF BRUTALISM[8]

Due to prejudice and unawareness brutalism as an architectural trend has been mostly devaluated, and the buildings that can be associated with it (most especially the non-Western ones) were until recently ignored or despised by European historians and their critical revisions of the 1980s. It was sometimes scornfully labeled as tardo-modern, a term used as a despicable tag. Its use was accepted only when applied to some very specific manifestations housed in Britain.[9]

Nevertheless, the large quantity of good quality examples, designed almost at the same time and proliferating in the five continents, with a remarkable similarity of architectural forms, materials, structural propositions and even programmatic discourses, can also be correctly labeled as fitting into the same pervasive and spread trend, and it is not illegitimate to call it brutalism. A trend that had perhaps conformed another international style, due to its very consistent flourishing, all over the world, in the 1950s-80s

moment, and as it seems, no clear or neat temporal precedence from the works of any other country.

It is undeniably that the brutalist trend produced, especially after the 1970s, several bad qualities, bad maintenance pieces of architecture sometimes with exaggerated structures and more frequently, lacking a sensible concern towards their surroundings. But it would be too hasty and shallow to condemn all brutalist interesting achievements for the sake of its deceptions. Besides – and paradoxically enough – some typical brutalist bias still survives, subtly but verifiably, in many contemporary architectures of the 21st century; and some of its discursive and formal paradigms still influences the architectural learning and academic practice patterns. And all that, despite the virtual absence of a more concerted analysis of its contribution in the canonical reference books thoroughly used around the world. But without reconsidering at some length the brutalist trend it would not be possible to properly understand contemporary architecture and the continued vitality of its modern roots.

As similarly happens in other countries and places, contemporary Brazilian architecture is indebted with the mid-20th century local brutalist manifestations (and also, with its international connections), and should be better studied as a necessary step that paves the way between classical modernity and present and modern-oriented contemporary architecture.

In Reyner Banham's writings[10] and in several others erudite (and even in less well-informed discussions) the term brutalism – in its broader international sense – is often superimposed with the so-called new brutalism movement – that was not perhaps such a good name for an exclusively or limited British circumstance. The term new brutalism was adopted perhaps with no precise program, but more probably as an anti- position, by a young generation of British architects and critics of the immediate postwar period. It was intended to loosely designate a state of dissatisfaction with the local and international state of affairs and to counterpoint the ongoing tension between continuity and transformation of the modernist tradition. That was the proper sense in which architects Alison and Peter Smithson used it, in their scarce and most synthetic texts that were published around 1955.

Banham and his colleagues of *Architectural Review* subsequently endorsed the phrase exaggerating its importance; and James Stirling mentioned the phrase in his brief account of Britain's immediate post-war architectural debates.[11] In that context and at that moment of the mid-1950s, it was by no means a style – but neither it was a concerted movement, since it lasted but a season, for the Smithsons' effusive creativity soon dragged them to other debates and propositions. The new brutalism would, given other circumstances, have been put out of all minds as just another historical curiosity, one among others in that moment's several debates. It was only one decade after, in the mid 1960s, that Banham's clever use of the Smithsons' names and positions bolstered the term in order to confound it with the brutalism as a world-wide spread trend – with the not innocent purpose of claiming the British precedence of the use.

But although Banham was very successful in his task of building a skewed historiography of brutalism, the precedence obviously belongs to Le Corbusier's works, whose lessons were being quickly learned by a worldwide network of his direct or indirect disciples. So that, as early as the end of the 1940s and the beginning of the 1950s and onwards, in many countries and places around the world, there began to appear in the architectural scenario some very significant and interesting brutalist works; although they were seldom labeled as that before the end of that decade and beginning of the 1960s.

The adoption of a brutalist idiom was the mingling result of different, and sometimes contradictory aspirations: Discourses on the necessity of industrialization combined with the use of carefully designed and handmade formworks; the necessity to improve the civil construction technical level and the use of abundant and non-specialized manual labor; the influence of Le Corbusier's new massive raw concrete formworks and plastic detailing mixed with the lightness and precision of Mies van der

Rohe's great-spans, porticoes structures. Many young architects from many places around the world converged to Le Corbusier's atelier in Paris and they brought back to their homes his influence and the desire to explore the plastic possibilities of reinforced and pre-tensed concrete. Even the worldwide increase of steel bars production may be considered as another condition that did not determine, but enabled the extensively use of reinforced and pre-stressed concrete structures, not only in big important commissions but even in more discrete situations, like individual houses, collective housing, office buildings and social equipment, among other programs.

From about 1960 onwards, there happens an exponential increase of the use of raw concrete on different types of buildings being constructed all around the world, designed by prestigious architects, whose work were disseminated by the free circulation of specialized journals and magazines and the increasing easiness of traveling abroad. In very few years Brutalism spread everywhere, taking the lead of its better examples, designed by some well-known masters and was confirmed as one of the most recognizable of that moment architectural tendencies. It emerged quite quickly as a more or less systematized *quasi-style*, easily recognizable and effortlessly adopted by other architects, with more or less ingenuity in each case. Supported and validated by the initial exemplary works of the 1950s and latter quickly established a recognizable idiom, a wide variety of brutalist works were published in several magazines around the world in the 1960s-70s – although they were quite never mentioned in the immediate posterior so-called *critical historiographies* of the 1980s.

Revising those examples, it can be perceived the existence of a relatively varied range of formal possibilities inside the brutalist trend; but it nevertheless showed significant common traces, especially in

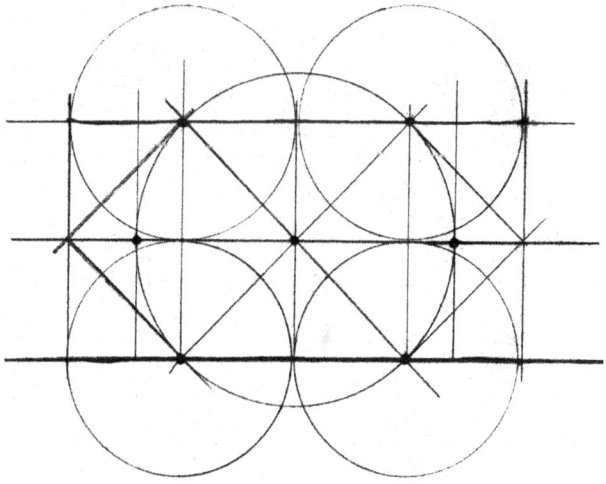

Jardim Calux Center for Child Education, geometric construction scheme, São Bernardo do Campo SP. Paulo Mendes da Rocha, 1972. Drawing Ruth Verde Zein

the visual and constructive domains. The first explicit statements acknowledging some architectural works as having a brutalist affiliation began to appear after 1959. They were rarely originated from the architects themselves, and came more frequently from commentators and critics; who based their assessments on a detailed description of the works, and not on an a priori body of doctrine – even if there are, in some cases, a few timid attempts in that vein.

When Reyner Banham organizes his belated 1966 book on brutalism the situation had completely changed, since his initial writings of the early 1950s concerning the local British new brutalism infatuation. There was already a multinational spreading of the brutalist tendency, which was quickly becoming one of the predominant architectural idioms most in use at the 1960s. Banham very clearly realizes that the field has changed and by no means brutalism could be seen as exclusively belonging to him and his friends. Nevertheless, he strives to convince the reader of the mythic British and Swedish origin of brutalism, and extends his sometimes-fallacious arguments to prove such precedence, mostly on the first half of his book. But in the second part of the book he also suggests the factual existence of an international *brutalist connection* – a very clever and precise assertion. Although Banham says that he "cannot explain its origin,"[12] he gives as reference several examples coming from many countries from Japan to Italy to Chile. And he declares that such brutalist connection works scattered in many places and continents cannot have been explained as originated from the British brutalist ideas and works, and that, brutalism as a world-wide tendency had no central origin – except, of course, Le Cobusier's propositions.

Unfortunately, what until now survived from Banham's critical contribution was not his clever brutalist connection survey, but mostly the prejudices and misinformation he puts forward in the first half of his book, which are still being quoted, in a quite un-critical way, by a large quantity of canonical and secondary books all over the world. It is a pity that, until now, Banham's contribution on the subject has being shrunk to the quoting of his biased pro-British deception, and do not mention the broad-minded cleverness of his international survey.

**ANYWAY, THE PHRASE BRUTALIST
CONNECTION, ALSO COINED BY BANHAM,
KEEPS ON BEING VERY USEFUL:**

> It attempts to give account of the simultaneous flourishing in several countries and regions of the world, of works in tune with a brutalist canon that was being quickly put up by means of the exemplary buildings designed by several architects practicing in many different countries that were not necessarily affiliated to

one another, or sharing a central focus – except, as above said, of a Corbusian origin – thus conforming an international network or connection. Indeed, brutalism was quite enthusiastically embraced, at some point in their careers, by virtually all the architects working in the 1960s and 1970s.[13]

Given the lack of recent scholarly, balanced accounts, brutalism continues to be seen, used and quoted in a confuse way; and that impedes its recognition as an important phenomenon in the architectural history of the mid-twentieth century. Such absence was perhaps also a consequence of rapid decline. Already by the end of the 1970s, brutalism began to be despised and even execrated, both by laymen and by the critical surveys of modern architecture written from the 1970s onwards – in both cases often with well-considered reasons.[14] Having been largely employed in the 1960s-70s to design public and official buildings, brutalism was labeled both by later neoliberal critics and by influential architectural historians as part of a mistaken and miscarried moment, both aesthetically and politically. Thus, for good or bad reasons, brutalist as a mid-20th century architectural trend has never received the attention it deserves, let alone a systematic assessment of its contribution. In short, most scholarly-oriented authors either rely on Banham without giving the matter much thought; in a few cases they are hostile towards it; but most frequently, they just ignore it.

THE SUPERFICIALITY OF THE TERM BRUTALISM

The absence of more systematic definitions of the term brutalism, despite its frequent, if imprecise application to certain modern architectural expressions of the mid-twentieth century, is paradoxical. Is then this term so vague that, in the end, it is not even worth an attempt to employ it in a coherent and consistent manner?

According to William Curtis,[15] neither postmodernism nor brutalism is easily characterized as a neatly delineated *style*, although each term is capable of designating a group of aspirations and rejections, however vague they may be. However, it does not seem so difficult to list brutalist characteristics, as they can be easily extracted from the ample range of works to which the term has been applied, and thus it is not hard to identify which works are, or seem to be, or at least might plausibly be seen as brutalist. Nor is it hard to list their formal, constructive, and even symbolic characteristics. What seems to slip through one's fingers is a way to grasp, among so many and such diverse production, something more than their likeness, something beyond a certain tactile sensibility. As Curtis states, the only thing, which really links brutalist architectures, is captured in a cliché, namely that "this architecture was the exposed concrete surface, obtained with the help of rough timber formwork."[16] Yet, this is insufficient to define brutalism as a tendency, let alone a style – considering that there also exist brutalist buildings made of brick masonry. The term brutalist seems to be inappropriate because it lacks any essential quality or substance, capable of linking beyond any doubt the majority of its manifestations. Such an essential quality might perhaps be *ethic*, or at least, a moral standard applied to architectural design. However, this would not be a definition, but a subterfuge, escaping from the vagueness of one domain – architecture – to the even greater vagueness of another – the ethical-moral dominion – leaving architecture to enter the dominion of philosophy, without solving our problem of defining it in architectural terms.

HOWEVER, INSTEAD OF DISCARDING BRUTALISM AS AN INAPPROPRIATE, CONCEPTUALLY VAGUE TERM WE MIGHT FIND THAT IT IS PARADOXICALLY SUITABLE, ONCE WE ADOPT A PRAGMATIC OR PHENOMENOLOGICAL APPROACH TO UNDERSTAND IT.

All one has to do is to renounce the search for an internal, essential harmony between brutalist works and accept, instead, that what really unites them is their appearance. If we accept this *superficial* definition and cease to look for an *essential* one, then we can, without logical inconsistency, bestow the title brutalist on a group of correctly dated works, sharing similar formal and surface characteristics, even though each one of them and/or their creators might display different conceptual, ethical and moral attitudes, in this way allowing for the variety of potential candidates for this designation. In other words, some buildings can be called brutalist simply because they appear to be so, since what determines their inclusion in the group is not their inner essence but their external surface; not their intrinsic characteristics but their extrinsic manifestations.

If such definition is acceptable, there is no conceptual problem in labeling some manifestations of a Brazilian *paulista* architecture of the 1950s and 1960s as brutalist, and to insert its contribution among other – and also forgotten - brutalist manifestations around the world.

SOME ASPECTS OF THE BRUTALISM CONTRIBUTION TO BRAZILIAN MODERN ARCHITECTURE TRADITION

The internationally consecrated narrative about Brazilian modern architecture acknowledges a collection of exceptional works, born in the 1930s from chance and genius, abruptly ending with Brasília's inauguration in 1960. Fifty years late, and despite recent books trying to further develop the subject, Brazilian architecture remains, for the majority of the foreigner observers, framed in the same frozen images of a glorious past suddenly stopped by a perplexing void. The so-called *critical revisions* of modern architecture, mostly written by Europeans in the 1980s, maintained the fiction by ignoring other possible interesting issues, works and architects in Brazil; pausing at the same B&W stills of Brasília's construction site, they do not even bother to actually visit the place and recheck their assumptions. With the growing distance in time such wornout stationary ideas do not suffice anymore. But although the situation demands a proper revision, it should not be carried on with as to generating new myths to be incrusted above former old ones; neither it is sufficient to praise new enlarged list of local geniuses to substitute or to side with the old consecrated ones.

Anyway, as above said, this article aim is not to achieve a renovated complete overview of Brazilian modern tradition. It modestly proposes to enforce some conceptual ideas concerning some interesting aspects of the mid-20th century modern architecture in Brazil and elsewhere; hoping that the present considerations would be able to open up and break apart the superficial, linear and triumphal accounts of Brazilian architecture. Its task is to collaborate to try and build a more complex, multi-layered and internationally connected critical historiography, able to praise our modern tradition and also, to surpass it when necessary; and such task can only be accomplished with the help of several other hands and minds, through lengthy and concerted researches.

In recent decades, the relative depletion of the post-modern critique against classical modernity gave room to a more sympathetic evaluation of its results. The 1950s-60s modern architecture is nowadays being progressively reconsidered and is found to be a more complex, ambiguous and valuable heritage than it was previously stated.[17]

Moreover, some of the brutalist works of the 1950s-70s and some of its more considered authors are now being appraised by a blossoming neo-modern (and sometimes, neo-brutalist) generation of architects. Contemporary pluralistic approaches expanded the floor admitting other perceptions and sensibilities, and some subjects, previously labeled as non-relevant, may now be included to compose an intensely varied, broad and multifarious panorama.

With such opening horizons in mind, one can ask again what have happened to Brazilian architecture after (and before) Brasília that remains unseen and unheard of. It seems that a fertile way of surpassing the common but sometimes imprecise interpretations concerning the decades of 20th century is to revise that panorama from its bare facts, in order to avoid the ideological bias of the discourses assuming a position against tardo-modernity and to drop the curfews that such label stated.

Brazilian modern architecture of the years 1935-60 (or the so-called *carioca* school) was rightly acclaimed on the immediate post-WWII due to its timely international diffusion, magnified by the void of that reconstruction moment and grounded on its truly excellent results. After becoming worldwide famous, it remained paradoxically hostage of a mythical narrative: As an inexplicable exception, as a fancy *modern baroque* style, as an exception born from geniality and chance. Such frozen narrative is being thoroughly revised by several Brazilian and foreign authors who are consistently composing a broader but also less superficial panorama. In any case, the prestige gained abroad by the *carioca* school rebounded home through the amplification of its importance and influence inside the country. After 1945 it begins to be accepted as the mainstream modern trend, a situation that helped to assure its nominal predominance inside the country at least until the construction of Brasília (1957-60).

In the beginning of the 1950s in Brazil and all around the world architects and architectures showed a remarkable apparent homogeneity of opinions and designs, which seemed to signalize the triumph of the modern ideals, as sorted out and proclaimed by the organic critics of modern movement. But under the outward happy show several profound divergences were concealed, different references were being used; distinct attitudes and aims were at stake.[18] All that situation was concocting many undercurrents that would sprout to full life only in the following decades, when the divergences became more clear; but then, they cannot be fully explained unless one looks, with keen eyes, to the underside of that previous apparent unanimity.

According to Comas,[19] the years 1935-45 represent the consolidation of the *carioca* school; the next decade, the dissemination of its lessons to other Brazilian regions. But already in the end of the 1940s and in the beginning of the 1950s, in Brazil and abroad, there starts a rising dissention against some of its superfluity traits. Although most of those critiques can be seen today as biased and prejudiced, some substratum lasted – and was perhaps quite convenient to assure the particular *paulista* mood favoring a drier, simplified and engineer-oriented architecture – as against the apparently superficial, hedonistic and formalist *carioca* architecture. Simultaneously, in the early 1950s some of the *carioca* school architects have already started to change their language and to explore new routes: Be it in the simpler and direct volumetric examples developed by Oscar Niemeyer from the Parque do Ibirapuera ensemble in São Paulo (1951-53) on; be it in the example of Affonso Eduardo Reidy precocious use of large rough concrete structures, as in the Brazil-Paraguay Elementary School (Asunción, Paraguay, 1952) and in the MAM RJ headquarters (Rio de Janeiro, 1953), both works of a brutalist language of magnified external transversal porticoes in exposed concrete.

Appearing in the scenario at approximately the same time, the rising *paulista* brutalist trend, supported by a talented new generation of local architects with the opportune alliance of some elder masters, begins to turn the game of prestige. From a few special and scattered works in the 1950s the trend expands exponentially in the 1960s to assume a prominent position inside Brazilian architectural panorama. Anyway, the country's architectural community never completely or pacifically accepts such predominance, even when its influence was accepted and spread to other regions and architects, reaching a peak in the mid-1970s.

After 1961, some of these architects and works were beginning to be labeled as brutalists: As before said, it was a title shared, but not necessarily accepted, by many others architects and works in Brazil and several countries all over the world. Scanning again that panorama, some good reasons for that label can be found, mostly, the notable likeness among all so-called brutalist works and their similar timing, no matter where they were. In almost any country a few but significant brutalist examples can be identified in the 1950s, a virtuoso crescendo can be perceived in the 1960s; in the 1970s there happens a reiterative repetition and aggrandizement of its formulas quickly exhausting the initial creative impulse into a mannerist stylized attitude. This last moment was, with good reasons, much despised by the 1980s critical revisions; that nevertheless preferred to throw the baby out with the bath water, by ignoring the best brutalist examples for the sake of the worst.

Even accepting the name brutalism as a handy label to visually gather many different works spread in Brazil and elsewhere, it still cannot be easily labeled, neither here nor there, as a steady movement sharing a homogeneous ethical point of view. Notwithstanding, it can surely be perceived as a most homogenous *quasi-style* – for perhaps the only bond all brutalist buildings share is just what one easily sees when looking from a predominately aesthetic and plastic point of view.

Although Banham only mentions one Latin American work in his belated comprehensive and highly controversial book on brutalism he makes an effort to include as much different examples from different places as possible. As about Latin America, he only mentions one outstanding Chilean example and do not included some Mexican, Argentinian or Brazilian brutalist works that would also perfectly fit in his broad sweeping of brutalist connection examples.

The absence of an international acknowledgment of the status and importance of the Brazilian *paulista* brutalist architecture of the 1957-75 in its moment, and until very recently, pairs with a similar lacking in the internal discourses that did not officially accept its importance until the appearance of a new generation of local critics working in the two last decades of the 20th century.

But such absence could keep on being disregarded as just another meaningless local episode, if not for the fact that the existence and importance of the *paulista* brutalism must be granted, not only for the sake of the historical register, but for the sheer quality of its buildings. And since the majority of them are still in use; and because their maintenance and transformation are stricken by several debates, their status as a high quality modern heritage examples must be assured, in order to guarantee their usefulness and preservation.

Positioned in the historiographical no-man's land between classical modern *carioca* school and the contemporary neo-modern Brazilian architecture, Brazilian brutalism – and mostly, but not exclusively, its *paulista* experiences – can be seen as a kind of *missing link* – and it is not the only one. But as stated above, it is not sufficient to give praises to some of its creators: Such attitude is just a disguised continuation of the same frozen, quasi-mythical scene until very recently displayed to roughly explain Brazilian modern architecture. An attitude that is here denounced as an insufficient and superficial account.

BESIDES BRUTALISM IS NOT THE ONLY STORY THAT IS MISSING: FOR A MORE COMPLETE REVISION IT WOULD BE ALSO NECESSARY TO ACKNOWLEDGE THE EXISTENCE OF A MULTIPLICITY OF OTHER SIMULTANEOUS TRENDS

and a variety of names and contributions. What can be said is that the 1950s-70s *paulista* brutalist trend is, for sure, a seminal contribution; and that, for better or for worse, contemporary Brazilian architecture derives equally from both the *carioca* and the *paulista* trends, and perhaps, even more from the second.

Paradoxically enough, although the *paulista* brutalist architecture clearly proposed a remarkable change, and a perhaps necessary renewal of Brazilian architectural panorama, its main protagonists chose, during the first decades of its consolidation and expansion, to omit their own evident dissatisfaction with its predecessors and to state their full political alliance with them – a dangerous mixture of architectural and political discourses that were fully complicated by the negative impacts of the military dictatorship affecting Brazil after 1964. Even if their works were in fact, although covertly, questioning the previous Brazilian modernity achievements, they do not feel at easy to state that. Perhaps, fearing one of the consequences of their independence;

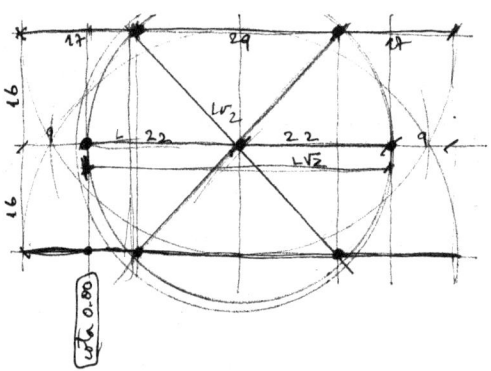

Jardim Calux Center for Child Education, geometric construction scheme, São Bernardo do Campo SP. Paulo Mendes da Rocha, 1972. Drawing Ruth Verde Zein

meaning, the breaking apart of a Brazilian modern architecture identity as a fixed trope, defined and congealed with the help of inside and abroad narratives); specially in a moment (1960s-70s) when it seemed necessary to be professionally united to confront the adverse political situation. The fact that such an internal disciplinary crisis coincided in time with such a bad political moment was a burden from which we have not yet completely recovered. But after half a century, and in the absence of the hostile political situation of that moment, the maintenance of a discourse holding a univocal *national identity* of Brazilian modern architecture strongly marked Brazilian architecture and architects, is neither satisfactory nor acceptable anymore.[20]

NOTES

EN. Article previously published at: Ruth Verde Zein, "Brazilian Architecture, Modern Tradition, Contemporary Culture. Other Brazilian Modernities of the 1950-70's," in: *Non West Modernist Past: on Architecture & Modernities*, eds. William Lim and Jiat-Hwee Chang (Cingapura: World Scientific Publishing, 2011), 169-180.

1. Sigfried Giedion, *Space, Time and Architecture. The Growth of a New Tradition* (Cambridge: The Harvard University Press, 1941).

2. The international recent publications are mostly in debt with local Brazilian studies that were held and published in Portuguese since the 1980s to-day; in fact, it could not exist without that basis of local cultural debates. Such books are very convenient to further divulgate Brazilian architecture abroad, *breaking the fast* to English-reading people. But they do not necessarily represent – as it happened in the mid-decades of 20th century writings on Brazil – the innovative tip of the critic, on the contrary.

3. A more extensive attempt was organized in our book: Maria Alice Junqueira Bastos and Ruth Verde Zein, *Brasil: arquiteturas após 1950* (São Paulo: Perspectiva, 2010).

4. The subject is further explored at the author's "Report on Brazil" article published at Heerle & Schmitz, 2009 (pages 44-at the section

"The birth of a nation: nature and geniality" (that text was written and first published on-line in Tu Berlin Habitat Unity website on Architecture & Identity conference, 2003, nowadays discontinued). Ruth Verde Zein, "Report on Brazil," in: *Constructing Identity in Contemporary Architecture. Case Studies from the South*, eds. Peter Heerle and Stephanus Schmitz (Munster: LIT Verlag, 2009), 37-86.

5. For further considerations on this subject, see Maria Alice Junqueira Bastos, *Pós-Brasilia, rumos da arquitetura brasileira* (São Paulo: Perspectiva, 2002); Bastos and Zein, *Brasil*.

6. The task of proposing an ample and concerted overview of Brazilian architecture of the second half of the 20th century was also realized by the author at a recently published book. Bastos and Zein, *Brasil*.

7. The international survey held since 2011 comprehends visitation, photography and studies of more than two hundred brutalist works, without exclusive emphasis on the American continent.

8. The factual demonstration of all the affirmations here displayed was thoroughly done with all academic rigor at the author's PhD dissertation, along with the quotation of all sources consulted, from period magazines, journals and books to more recent criticism. For the sake of the brevity and lightness they are not reproduced here but may be consulted at: Ruth Verde Zein, "A arquitetura da escola paulista brutalista 1953-1973" (PhD diss., UFRGS, 2005), http://www.lume.ufrgs.br/handle/10183/5452.

9. Very recent books are still insisting on repeating the same old stories, showing a complete lack of understanding of the international spreading and importance of the Brutalism outside Britain and everywhere, insisting the unsustainable myth of its local – mostly British – origin and precedence. Despite their interest as a local study case, its conclusions cannot be hastily extrapolated to comprise all the field; as so, they perpetuate the misinformation, born from simple ignorance, lack of a broader research, and last but not least, Eurocentric prepotency. This is the case, for example, of: Alexander Clement, *Brutalism. Post-War British Architecture* (Rambsbury: Crowood Press, 2010).

10. See Reyner Banham, "The New Brutalism," *Architectural Review* 708, 1955; Reyner Banham, *The New Brutalism. Ethic or Aesthetic?* (London: Architectural Press, 1966).

11. James Stirling, "Regionalism and Modern Architecture," *Architect's Year Book* 7, 1967, 62-68. Reproduced in: Joan Ockman, ed., *Architecture Culture 1943-1968. A documentary anthology* (New York: Rizzoli, 1993), 242-248.

12. Banham, *The New Brutalism*, 135.

13. This affirmation is based on a broad, international survey now in course by the author, using mostly period publications, the Access of original drawings on library and archives that are being consulted in all the American continent (from Canada to Chile), plus some other initial surveys with the help of friends on other parts of the world. It is very important to consult the original publications, since many architects, when producing their own comprehensive books about their works sometimes tend to *forget* or excise the works of their brutalist moment.

14. Mainly due to maintenance problems, exaggerated initial costs, and poor environmental performances. In defense of these buildings one could say that they tended to be experimental, and in consequence, more subject to previously unknown problems. It is important to correct those errors – but that do not allow to indiscriminately disregard all brutalist buildings for the sake of the worst ones.

15. William Curtis, *Modern Architecture since 1900* (London: Phaidon, 1996), 602.

16. Ibid., 434.

17. See: Sarah Williams Goldhagen and Réjean Legault, *Anxious Modernisms. Experimentation in Postwar Architectural Culture* (Quebec: Canadian Centre for Architecture/MIT, 2000).

18. Goldhagen and Legault, *Anxious Modernisms*.

19. Carlos Eduardo Dias Comas, "Precisões brasileiras. Sobre um estado passado da arquitetura e urbanismo modernos" (PhD diss., Université de Paris VII, 2002).

20. As a short notice it would worth mentioning some of the *paulista* brutalist best works and authors. From around 1957 on, the *paulista* brutalism contributed to Brazilian architecture with several important works. In the early 1950s the architects João Batista Vilanova Artigas (1915-84) and Carlos

MODERN TRADITION
AND CONTEMPORARY CULTURE

Cascaldi gradually begin to use exposed concrete structures, such as the Morumbi Stadium (1952), in São Paulo, or the Olga Baeta Residence (1956), also in São Paulo. As well as Artigas, other mature architects at that moment started to adopt the brutalist language in their works, from the late 1950s onward: as did the architect Lina Bo Bardi (1914-92), when designing Museu de Arte de São Paulo – MASP (1958-61); Fabio Penteado (n.1928), in the headquarters of the Harmonia Club (1964); Carlos Barjas Millan (1927-64), in the Roberto Millan Residence (1960); Telésforo Cristófani (1929-2003), in the Fasano Vertical Restaurant (1964) and Hans Broos (n.1921), in the Saint Boniface's Parish Center (1965). A new generation of newly graduated architects starts a career contributing to the consolidation of the *paulista* face of the brutalist trend in the end of the 1950s. Names as Paulo Mendes da Rocha (n.1928), in the Paulistano Club (1958); Joaquim Guedes (1932-2008), in the Cunha Lima Residence (1959); Francisco Petracco (n.1935) and Pedro Paulo de Mello Saraiva (1933-2016) in the Clube XV in Santos (1963); Paulo Bastos (n.1936), in the São Paulo Military Headquarters (1965); Pedro Paulo de Mello Saraiva with Sami Bussab (n.1939) and Miguel Juliano e Silva, with the Ballroom of the Syria-Lebanon Club (1966); Ruy Othake (n.1938) in Tomie Ohtake Residence (1966) and in the Central Telefônica Campos do Jordão (1973); João Walter Toscano (n.1933), in the Health Resort in Águas de Prata SP (1969); among many others.

BR   LATIN AMERICA: CRITICAL
5   THOUGHTS   READINGS

LATIN AMERICAN CONTEMPORARY ARCHITECTURE

COMMON SENSE AND IDEALISM

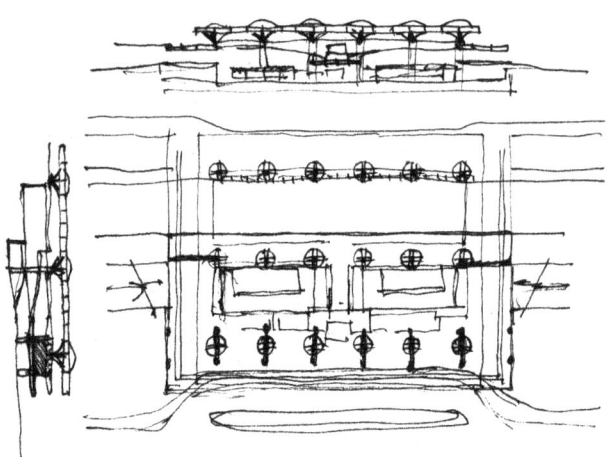

Jaú Bus Station, section of the ramps and first floor plan, Jaú SP.

Vilanova Artigas, 1973. Drawing Ruth Verde Zein

Latin America is almost a continent,[1] encompassing dozens of countries and a varied assortment of cultural, political and geographical realities. As so, it is a very difficult task to find just one building apt to represent the diversity and complexity of its contemporary architecture. Yet, that was exactly the briefing presented by the organizers to the participants of the International Committee of Architectural Critics – CICA Shanghai 2015 Seminar. Certainly, to represent our subcontinent, it would be easy to choose one building among several other slightly familiar contemporary buildings that had already been published in one of the main international magazines and websites. Instead, I have preferred to select a not so well known, quite small and low-key piece of architecture. I believe that was a good choice, and that this building – the Projeto Viver headquarters in São Paulo, Brazil – is a perfect case. Among other reasons, because it allows me to introduce some meaningful and interesting contemporary debates, that are constantly permeating the ever-changing conditions of our urban and architectural realities in Latin America – and perhaps, elsewhere.

Projeto Viver building won in 2014 a very important Latin American Architecture Award. It is a prize that has been created in 2013, and it is still little known outside the continent, but its importance and acceptance will exponentially increase in the next decade. It is organized and granted by the Rogelio Salmona

Foundation, whose headquarters are situated in Bogotá, Colombia; and its name is "Rogelio Salmona Latin American Architecture Award: Open spaces/collective spaces."

Before describing how this award was created, and how the competition to choose the winner is being organized, it is necessary to explain who was Rogelio Salmona (1929-2007). Born in France, his family migrated to Colombia when he was very young. His excellent drawing skills and superior talent were early recognized: He was appointed to work with Le Corbusier for his plan to Bogotá when he was still a student of architecture. In 1948 he moved to Paris and joined Le Corbusier's rue de Sèvres atelier. He lived in France for a decade, having travelled all through Europe and beyond. When he returned to Colombia in 1958 his works revealed a personal critical approach to architecture, permeated by a more attentive regard to the local necessities and resources of each region and urban context. His attitude was in resonance with that of other Latin American creators of his generation, as for example, Eladio Dieste in Uruguay or Carlos Mijares in Mexico, all of them considered by some historiographical revisions on Latin America architecture as representing another modern trend, the *appropriate* modernity.[2] Salmona strongly believed that the design of any piece of architecture had to be treated as an opportunity to enrich the quality and livability of the city. His works always strived to include public open spaces that positively contributed to a more friendly and democratic city. Finally, world-widely critics and historians recognize Salmona as one of the most important Latin America's third generation modern architects.

After his demise, the Rogelio Salmona Foundation, established in Bogotá, Colombia, is preserving his legacy. They launched in 2013 the "Rogelio Salmona Latin American Architecture Award: Open spaces/collective spaces," to further celebrate his memory. The first edition of the biannual award happened in 2014, and the second edition was launched and was completed in 2016.[3] The Prize mission is to identify, recognize and stimulate the dissemination of good architectural practices in Latin American and Caribbean cities. It seeks to put in value high-quality buildings that also generate significant and convivial open and collective spaces for the city and its inhabitants, thus contributing to the development and consolidation of more inclusive urban spaces.

A unique characteristic of this award is that it is granted only for buildings being used for at least five years, and are still in proper and good use at the moment of their selection for the competition. The award is granted either to public or to private buildings, provided that they stand out for the quality and generosity of their design. Buildings of any program, dimension or scale, may be nominated to the award, as long as their design conception had strived to include lasting and stimulant open collective spaces. The nominated buildings should be in use, thus giving evidence that their architectural spaces had actually been able to encourage the spontaneous gathering of citizens.

**IN BRIEF, THE AWARD PURPOSE IS
TO CELEBRATE BUILDINGS THAT ARE
COLLABORATING TO THE BETTERMENT OF
THEIR RESPECTIVE URBAN ENVIRONMENTS,
AND DOING SO IN A RESPECTFUL WAY:**

By recognizing and valuing its place, the surrounding architectural ambiance and the nearby urban life.

The Salmona Prize is not an open competition, although any person may submit suggestions at the Foundation's website. The buildings are selected, after careful consideration of all information available, by an international committee of experts, consisting of four members, representing Latin America's four main regions, helped by their respective local teams. In the 2014 the CICA co-founder, Mexican art and architecture critic Louise Noelle represented Central America and the Caribbean.

Colombian architectural historian and critic Silvia Arango, one of the founders of the Latin American Seminars – SAL, represented South America's Andean countries. Editor of *Summa+* magazine and architectural critic Fernando Diez, also a member of the Holcim Awards International Jury, represented deep South America countries. And I was in charge of the selection of works of the fourth so-called region, my country, Brazil.[4]

In the first edition of the prize, due to the combined efforts of the international committee experts and respective local teams, more than a hundred buildings built between 2000 and 2008 were carefully considered, studied and visited. Twenty-one buildings from Argentina, Chile, Colombia, Bolivia, Brazil, Ecuador, Mexico, Peru, Puerto Rico and Venezuela were selected for the 2014 Salmona Award. The authors were contacted by the Foundation, and those who had agreed to participate sent graphic material to organize an exhibition and a book, that are now circulating thorough Latin America. The final jury included the four already mentioned international committee experts plus a fifth juror, in order to give us a much needed foreign perspective. In the 2014 Salmona Award the guest juror was the Japanese architect Hiroshi Naito. After the careful reexamination of all candidates, and three days of intense debates, the jury decided to grant the prize, plus three honorable mentions.

It was a challenge to try and find well designed, contextually meaningful and well maintained Latin American buildings able to fulfill the award's requirements. But surprisingly, it was not as difficult as we initially thought it would be.[5]

In order to catch up with the 21st century, the Award first edition encompassed the buildings inaugurated between 2000 and 2008. The 2016 Award edition would include buildings inaugurated between 2008 and 2011; and so on. My support team in Brazil has already begun to track the examples to be considered for the 2016 Award, and for the next ones. It is early to say, but it seems that our task is going to become progressively easier in the years ahead.

WE HAVE THE FEELING THAT THERE IS PERHAPS A SPRINGING TREND GROWING AMONG LATIN AMERICA'S YOUNG AND EXPERIENCED ARCHITECTS: AN AIM TO CONTRIBUTE TO THE PRODUCTION OF MEANINGFUL PUBLIC SPACES FOR THE 21ST CENTURY CITIES.

Maybe this is just a wishful thinking. But let's hope my optimistic forecast is correct, and our *urban weather* is about to change for the better in the next decades, despite crises and difficulties that strive our subcontinent – or maybe, because of them.

LATIN AMERICAN RUTH VERDE ZEIN
CONTEMPORARY ARCHITECTURE

Considering the sheer diversity of situations and modalities that may be included in the apparently simple idea of *architecture that helps make city* – a lead that ably and briefly summarizes the award's feature and intention, the main difficult that we, the international committee members, had found, was how to better understand and sort out the meaningful examples. For us, it was quite clear that we were not dealing with the traditional, 19th century, European-born idea of the city. We tried to understand, to work with, and if possible, to praise, our Latin American cities for what they are, without burdening them with the heavy shadow of anachronistic conceptual ghosts, unfit to aptly understand our realities. As we know, Latin American cities are relatively new constructs of varied dimensions, huge contrasts, stark juxtapositions of scales and styles, formal and economical incongruities, informalities and discontinuities, with vast environmental and social problems on the one hand, and strong speculative and financial powers dominating the floor on the other hand. This complex mixture results in an apparently unbalanced ensemble of very difficult rational apprehension, and even more difficult and concerted solution. So, if we observe our cities with a hasty or biased look, we tend to be shocked, and to perceive them only as an amorphous set of uninteresting, dystopian and ugly objects isolated by obnoxious in-between voids made of debris or unconsolidated fabrics. If that were so, would there be any room for finding good meaningful contemporary buildings to be considered under the lead of *architecture that helps make city*?

Perhaps surprisingly, yes there was. In Brazil, in Latin America, we were actually able to identify a perhaps relatively small (considering the huge size of our cities), but still most significant number of exceptional buildings that deserved to be more carefully examined and considered for the Salmona Award. A few of these buildings were born from important governmental efforts; a number resulted from the initiative of non-governmental agencies, and several from generous initiatives of private agents. Some were buildings that had already been internationally well publicized; many others were somewhat discreet but very interesting examples, designed with huge doses of common sense, spiced with a pinch of idealism. Some were buildings inserted in prestigious parks and consolidated public spaces; others were found in dense central areas and neighborhoods; others, in the sprawling and precarious metropolitan peripheries. Some had been built with the benefit of large budgets; others had been erected with a very tight economy of means and resources. All of them were found randomly punctuating their respective cities. In any case, the selected works were also, or may I say, primarily, some very good pieces of architecture, since their esthetical qualities were not at all a secondary aspect of our selection criteria.

Each of these buildings was designed by one out of an ample variety of architects, of different generations, working

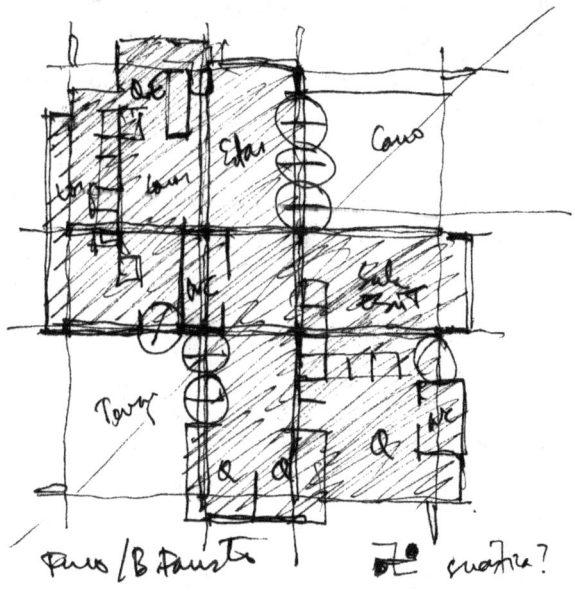

Boris Fausto Residence, ground floor plan, São Paulo SP. Sérgio Ferro, 1961. Drawing Ruth Verde Zein

in many different places of our large subcontinent. Yet, all the authors seemed to have worked on the possibility that their cities would perhaps experience some good changes with the help of the, sometimes very discreet, open spaces created by their buildings, even if they would affect the city only in a modest small scale. These works and sometimes their authors' discourses seemed to trust that a good example of a good architectural design, of an architecture that makes city, might be able to have a say, albeit small, in helping transforming and contaminating their places, for the better.

Perhaps, even if in a most inconspicuous way, all theses examples still carry on the old, almost burnt off, flame of utopia. I'm sorry to bring up here again this apparently outworn concept. But here, I do not want it to mean something fixed, like a set of closed ideas carrying a magical power that would suddenly and completely change forever and ever architecture, the cities and their inhabitants. The word utopia, here, is meant as a more simpler and modest concept. Or else, it is here used just to better characterize a challenging condition: The belief that there is still some possibility of changing the world for the better, even if punctually, even if only in our surroundings, even if just in minuscule doses; and that architecture may still have a say in that possible change, too. Which is exactly the belief that has primarily moved the organizers of the Rogelio Salmona Prize in the first place.

As it happens, I was very surprised when, after one of two days of debates, the members of the Salmona Award Jury gradually drifted into considering the possibility of choosing a Brazilian building as the winner of the 2014 edition of the prize. Although I considered it as a very fine example of architecture, it was not initially my favorite, but the Chilean examples. However, during the very interesting jury debates, by learning from each other's opinions and questionings, my position gradually changed.

EVENTUALLY, THE JURY MEMBERS REALIZED THAT IT WAS BETTER IF THE FIRST SALMONA PRIZE EDITION WOULD NOT GO TO A LARGE SCALE EXAMPLE, BUT INSTEAD, THAT IT SHOULD BE GRANTED TO A VERY MODEST AND INDEPENDENT EXAMPLE.

So we chose the Projeto Viver Building, in São Paulo, designed by FGMF Architects.[6]

It would be very interesting to carefully consider all twenty buildings that were selected for the 2014 Salmona Award; or at a minimum, the three honorable mentions.[7] But since the space here is limited, I will have to stick only to the prize winner. Alas, a careful consideration of the other buildings would better introduce the winner, in the sense that their features would help prepare the terrain to fully understand the qualities of Projeto Viver. If not for other reasons, because I would not like you to look at that building as an isolated piece of good architecture – which it certainly is. Besides looking at this building in itself, it should also be understood beyond that: As a sign of how Latin America 21st century cities should be thought of, and acted upon. In any case, if this building does not contain a simple or all-encompassing formula, it may contain a broad proposition: That in our half-consolidated cities, sometimes we have to think small to think big. In order to look at this building – and to our Latin American cities – for what they are, and for what they could be, we have to sail away from the moorings of previous centuries, European-born ideologies, and to get stripped of all such petty prejudices. In many ways, this modest building represents a possible and fruitful future – but we have to refresh our eyes to fully realize that.

The Projeto Viver building is situated in the Morumbi neighborhood of São Paulo city, an area that contains side by side both luxury villas and condominiums and popular housing and informal slums. Projeto Viver building was designed to serve the underprivileged population from the deprived Jardim Colombo community (*favela*). It hosts the activities of the non-governmental organization "Viver em Família" (Living in Family Association), whose mission is to help the human development of that community. The 30m x 50m lot was the last open area available in the vicinity, and was formerly misused as an illegal garbage disposal place. Despite that insalubrious condition, it was daily crossed by the *favela* residents in order to access the internal streets of the neighborhood, and precariously used as a common living area for playing soccer and other social events of the community. Right from the very start, the architects of the Projeto Viver building acknowledged these features from their better side, and strived to maintain the place open for the free crossing and the leisure of the neighbors. Their first step to define the *parti* was to adequately redesign the preexisting accesses for vehicles and pedestrians. Instead of the existing sloppy and ravenous terrain, the Projeto Viver building and its open spaces defined a multi-leveled square, saving the gap between the public street and the favela. As so, the center of the terrain is not occupied by the constructions, but to be freely used for resting, an open plaza for contemplation, children's games, and the bleachers for open air shows.

The functional program itself was split into two pavilions. A longitudinal pavilion is placed next to the western limit of the

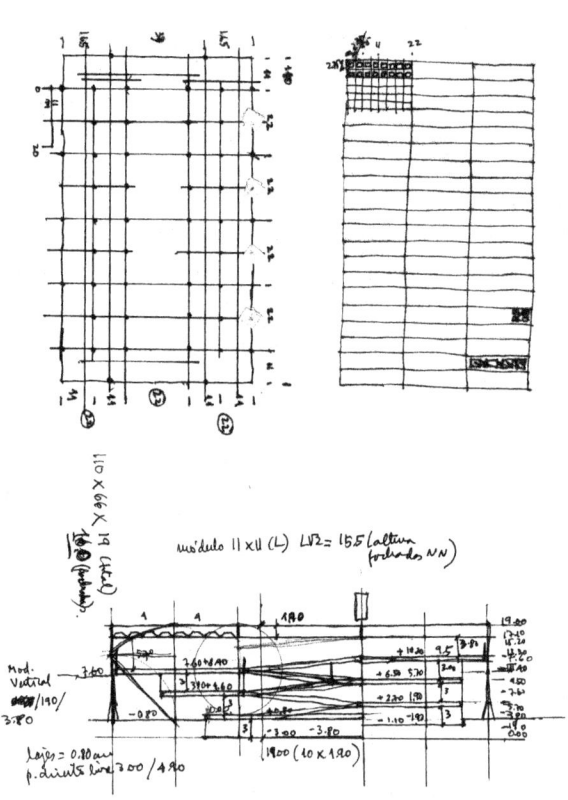

School of Architecture and Urbanism of USP, structural schemes and transverse section, São Paulo SP. Vilanova Artigas and Carlos Cascaldi, 1961. Drawing Ruth Verde Zein

parcel; a second pavilion is placed transversally, in the back, over pilotis, so as not to impair the crossing of people accessing the *favela*. Both pavilions define the public/open spaces, and organize them in two sectors: The graded plaza access and the lower flat multi-sports court. The pilotis of the second pavilion may be used as a kind of covered verandah where multiple programmed and/or informal activities may happen. The transversal pavilion houses above multipurpose rooms for classes, meetings and administrative uses and a small library. Underground, bellow the pilotis level, there is a basement with changing rooms and deposits that are used by the players and/or as a communal bathing facility, whose management is organized by the local neighbor's association. The longitudinal pavilion ground floor houses the reception, the janitor's house and a multi-disciplinary workshop with a large swinging door that may be used to open the premises to the public spaces, when necessary. On the upper floor there are compact rooms for medical, dental, legal and psychological care plus a waiting room. Facing the street there is also an experimental kitchen that is used for training classes open to the community. There is also a small shop open to the street that offers the possibility of selling the goods that are produced there. An upper garden terrace floor houses a small kid's playroom; it is open for supervised activities such as gardening, yoga etc. Anyway, the arrangement of the spaces is highly flexible, so nowadays, after some years of being in use, some of these activities have given room to others, according to the NGO and the community changing needs – as it was expected. The two pavilions are connected by elevated passageways, and the rooms on the upper floors, especially those meant to be used by the community, are very open and transparent, as to signalize that everyone is welcome, and to dispel the initial mistrust that could have arisen within the community, when the Projeto Viver Association initially moved to its headquarters.

The building structure is quite simple, using reinforced concrete and concrete block walls. The metal windows frames are sometimes protected by galvanized steel flap louvers, or else, with tilting metallic elements that may be closed to darken the room's interiors during day classes. The staircases and the metal walkways were made in an expanded metallic mesh system, as well as the overhead door of the workshop and the sealing perforated plates from the caretaker's house. The building construction intentionally employs simple and regular materials that are very commonly used in the poorer neighborhoods of the city, such as the concrete blocks and ceramic shards. But here these materials are disposed in a somewhat different and innovative way: The building integrates to the place, without imitating it, but seeking to propose its aesthetic requalification.

Finally, some words about the authors. This building was designed when the architects counted only five years of practice. In 2000 as young architects Fernando Forte, Lourenço Gimenes and Rodrigo Marcondes Ferraz founded FGMF Architects, and since then their firm has been steadily growing up. Today, fifteen years later, they have already developed 350 projects.[8] Despite the relatively large volume of projects, theirs is still a relatively small office, looking for opportunities to experiment as much as possible with different scales, materials and demands. Such diversity helps them keep their highly investigative performance and a healthy business management focused in design excellence and high productivity. They say they believe that the critical acceptance of the error is the key to a good design process: Such anti-formalistic or *erratic* behavior is perhaps what stimulates them to achieve a smart adaptability, which makes them able to cope with each different situation.

Latin America is almost a continent. It would be preposterous of me to even think about aptly representing its contemporary architecture with just one building. Anyway, I hope this quite small and low-key piece of architecture is also apt to show you something about our urban and architectural realities – as such, in the plural.

NOTES

EN. English version originally presented at the CICA-Shanghai Seminar (December 2015).

1. Brazil has 8.516.000 km², around 10% smaller than China (9.597.000 km²). Latin America's area (inclusive the Caribbean region) exceeds that of both together (21.070.000 km²).

2. Enrique Browne, *Otra Arquitectura en America Latina* (Mexico: Gustavo Gili, 1988); Marina Waisman and Cesar Naselli, *10 Arquitectos Latinoamericanos* (Sevilha: Dirección General de Arquitectura Y Vivienda, 1989); Antonio Toca, *Nueva Arquitectura en America Latina: Presente y Futuro* (Mexico: Gustavo Gili, 1990); Jorge Francisco Liernur, *America Latina. Architettura, gli Ultimi Vent'anni* (Milano: Electa Editrice, 1990); Cristian Fernandez Cox and Antonio Toca Fernandez, *America Latina: Nueva Arquitectura. Una Modernidad Posracionalista* (Mexico: Gustavo Gili, 1998); Hugo Segawa, *Arquitectura Latinoamericana Contenporánea* (Mexico: Gustavo Gili, 2005).

3. Fundación Rogelio Salmona, http://obra.fundacionrogeliosalmona.org/; Latin American Award, http://premio.fundacionrogeliosalmona.org/.

4. I also acted as Brazil's representative for the 2016 edition of the Salmona Prize. For the 2018 prize Brazil was represented by Alexandre Ribeiro Gonçalves.

5. The first edition of the prize embraced buildings inaugurated between 2000 and 2008. The 2016 edition selected buildings opened between

2008 and 2011. The 2018 edition considered buildings inaugurated until 2012, and so on.

6. Fernando Forte, Lourenço Gimenes and Rodrigo Marcondes Ferraz are partners at FGMF Architects.

7. Plus the nineteen works selected for the 2016 prize and so on... All of them interesting!

8. Until December 2015, when this text was originally written. The numbers are naturally in permanent update.

ZEIN, Ruth Verde
　　Critical Readings / Ruth Verde Zein; edited by: Abilio Guerra, Fernando Luiz Lara and Silvana Romano Santos. - São Paulo: Romano Guerra; Austin: Nhamerica, 2019.
　　258 p. : il. (Latin America: Thoughts; 5)

　　ISBN: 978-85-88585-77-5 (Romano Guerra)
　　ISBN: 978-1-946070-22-7 (Nhamerica)

　　　　1.Modern Architecture - critic 2.Modern Architecture - Latin America I.Guerra, Abilio, ed. II.Lara, Fernando Luiz, ed. III. Santos, Silvana Romano, ed. IV.Title V.Serie

　　　　　　　　　　　　　　　　　　　　　　　CDD 720.1

Dina Elisabete Uliana – CRB-8/3760

© Ruth Verde Zein

Translated from original edition *Leituras críticas*,
Ruth Verde Zein, 2018
ISBN: 978-85-88585-76-8 (Romano Guerra)
ISBN: 978-1-946070-20-3 (Nhamerica)

All rights reserved. Legally constituted exceptions aside, no part of this publication, including the cover design, may be reproduced, distributed, publicly transmitted or transformed by any means, electronic, chemical, mechanical, optical, tape recording or photocopy, without prior permission in writing from both the copyright holders and the Publisher. Infraction of the rights mentioned may constitute an infringement of intellectual copyright.

All rights reserved

Romano Guerra Editora
Rua General Jardim 645 cj 31
01223-011 São Paulo SP Brasil
rg@romanoguerra.com.br
www.romanoguerra.com.br

Nhamerica Platform
807 E 44th st.
Austin, TX, 78751 USA
editors@nhamericaplatform.com
www.nhamericaplatform.com

COVER IMAGE
Photo Ruth Verde Zein

This book was composed in Alegreya and Raleway
Printed in paper Offset 90g and Duodesign 250g

www.ingramcontent.com/pod-product-compliance
Lightning Source LLC
Chambersburg PA
CBHW052053110526
44591CB00013B/2196